INTEGRATION

of

THOUGHTS

FLORDELIZ CAYABAN-HACKETT, DBA

INTEGRATION

of

THOUGHTS

authorHOUSE®

AuthorHouse™
1663 Liberty Drive
Bloomington, IN 47403
www.authorhouse.com
Phone: 1-800-839-8640

First published by AuthorHouse   02/11/2012

ISBN: 978-1-4685-5186-0 (sc)
ISBN: 978-1-4685-5185-3 (ebk)

Printed in the United States of America

This book is printed on acid-free paper.

Share your love and bring hope to the diverse populace.

Contents

Acknowledgments

This writing I owe to the people that I met through jobs, seminars, volunteer work, business affiliations, surveys, and interviews—both academic and nonacademic, including those I encountered on the road. While everyone came from different backgrounds, each one was trying to understand the value of life and longing for compassion in a deeper way. The openness of conversations and experiences and practices in this book are very simple, and that makes ordinary people grasp every feature without hesitation.

I am thankful to pastors and missionaries from whom I always asked for spiritual guidance. I am also thankful to my friends of different cultures. I respect them for their kind hearts. I also thank those "hard people" from whom I learned the value of humility.

To my children, who give me courage to go on and who helped me in so many ways to complete this project, I want to say, *"I love you."* Your uniqueness helped to bring me to where I am now. You are all precious to me. My husband gives balance to my life; I thank you so much. I can't forget my parents, my sisters and brothers, to whom I gave my respect. They shelter me with their love which brings integrity to my life.

Most of all, to my Creator, our God who loves us: I'm giving Him all the glory and honor, for bringing me this far, for guiding me in the process and illuminating the power of His love.

Introduction

Young and old, conservative and liberals are talking about change. Change is an issue that saturates all areas of life. It is frequently driven by financial factors; it can be the result of a crisis, a changing market, or a changing technology. There are internal changes with positive external results. There are different drivers to consider. And in this book, change is focused on *cultural imperatives* and *leader and employee behavior*. I say that planning can predict change.

As a result of the collapse of communism,[1] the world changed, and the business world was not exempt from that change. There was a change in the economic and social standing of nations. Domestic firms found that their local markets could no longer increase revenue at their home office. Thus, businesses extended their services outside where foreign markets accepted the product, and they simultaneously included in their budgets the cost of the product so they could regularly enjoy the use of it. As an example, hygienic products and baby products are consumed in almost every family. In this case, the domestic firms insistently look globally for new markets. It does not end there. Services, as we can see, are rumbling around the world. Because of the open communication, services are open and fast to roam around.

Some corporations branched out to China, India, Indonesia, and even Vietnam, searching for an extension of sales. Brazil, along with

---

[1]   1991—Cold war was over.

other countries, at the other end collaborates in the practice of trade. Furthermore, more call centers were branched to the Philippines, competing and collaborating with those local long-distance carriers. More service organizations are networking and are accepted openly. Affiliation of schools and colleges are also sprouting like mushrooms. Everything is at our fingertips.

The expansion into new markets carries with it three major benefits. First, a firm may be able to realize economic balance, lowering average costs as its production increases. Second, the expansion results in the diversification of the firm's income. Third, trade border barriers are reduced or eliminated. As trade goes to more countries, the firm becomes less dependent on its sales in any one country. Eventually, leadership comes hand in hand in almost all countries. The World Trade Organization has opened doors to traders around the globe[2] and that is when culture becomes vulnerable to one another.

---

[2]   Canada's International Market Access Priorities 2001

Culture

Culture controls both the internal and external expansion of a business. It plays an important role in the movement of the workforce. Culture is known as a learned pattern of values, beliefs, behaviors, customs, and attitudes that distinguish one society, or as the unique lifestyle of a particular group of people Culture determines how each member communicates and interacts with others. Since culture is a learned behavior, the culture changes in response to external forces, the market, and the products and services that affect the society. Business, like all other human activities, is conducted within the context of society. Understanding and respecting the cultural differences among people will transform the direction of society and the business as well.

Chapter 1

Finding Balance:
Do We Need to Go Back
to the Basics?

Historically, the hierarchical model of management communication was reasonably popular until a series of economic, social, and technical changes forced a transformation in thinking about organization and industry. Much, if not most, of today's organizations undergoing rapid technological change, globalization, and expansion and/or contraction of establishments, require one who is able to collaborate effectively with their changing workforce and customers. Questions like these may arise very fast: How do we want our possessions to happen today? How do we want to produce? To succeed, we need to wake up to what works. Then every effort we make could be productive.

Strange as it seems, the millennial generation can text-message, surf the Internet, microwave a snack, listen to iTunes, and download a favorite TV show all at the same time—they call this multitasking. In addition, these same people can send images and text messages in Facebook, blog in Twitter, as well as see and speak to their friends and relatives on the other side of the world using Skype. Information, information, and more information! Something we had never dreamed of before.

Today, the traditional boundaries between politics, culture, technology, finance, national security, and ecology are rapidly disappearing. Every category is attached to the others. It is as if all of them are interconnected in one loop. As we further our journey, writers, researchers, and professionals look at the world through a multicultural, multipersonal perspective and communicate the complexity to everyone through simple stories, not theories. We call this change "leadership." Everyone is given the exceptional opportunity to climb to the top of one's chosen profession, regardless of where they started.

In 2000 BC and thereafter, we read Scriptures of leaders and simple men, telling parables and stories. This shows that the change we have now is a continuation of the past works of these leaders. As an example, there was a series of events that occurred in the 1970's. There were two friends who were inseparable. Although both attended the same college, they were in different departments; one was in education and the other was in accounting. After college, they were separated. Although both completed their undergraduate studies, one was successful in her career as an educator, but the other changed jobs often. After several years, the two friends met again. Both were eager to know what had happened to the other. The educator became concerned with the friend's situation and discussed the circumstances with another friend. This other friend was able to influence some businesses, and because she empathized with the situation, she was able to refer the first friend to a chief executive officer (CEO). And she got a job. After a few months in her new job, this person went back to the friend and asked what she could do to return the favor that had been extended to her. The answer was: move on. You have nothing to repay. And with all her heart, she thanked the friend for having a good heart.

Remembering this scenario, I also remember a story written in "Luke 10:30-37" (KJV) from the Holy Bible about the good Samaritan, who took care of a man wounded by thieves. The Good Samaritan, who had compassion for the injured man, brought him to an inn and took care of him. The following morning, he gave money to the host and asked him to take care of the man until he got well. On the other hand, Jesus healed the ten lepers, and one went back to thank Him (Luke 17:11-19, KJV). Pastors, who interpreted these two stories in various manners, preached the story of the Good Samaritan, and Jesus healing the ten lepers. And various listeners find themselves asking how many good Samaritans are there in this world and if there is more than one Jesus. And this story will be relayed to people again and again. Some will just close their eyes, hold their breath, and pray for a good Samaritan and Jesus to always be around. Although there are differences in interpretation, at the end it shows hope, and that compassion will find its way to help or guide others in every way of one's life. Thank you for the Good Samaritan and Jesus.

In the 1980's Maria arrived in Micronesia as a tourist. After a week of stay, Maria was on the road looking for a job. On her way to nowhere, she noticed a construction area. She stopped by and looked to see if somebody was around. Looking down, she noticed a carpenter fixing his tool. Maria greeted the man with a casual, "Good morning." The carpenter paused for a moment and looked at Maria.

"Please advise me where to get a domestic job," Maria asked. He looked at her and asked, "What was your occupation in the past?" Maria answered him in a very low voice and then stated, "I really need a job." (She was thinking of her ten children that she left in her home country.)

Without hesitation, the carpenter instructed Maria to go to the port and try her luck. "The accountant just left his position, and they need someone to replace him," he continued. At that moment, Maria was very happy.

Now she needed to find a ride. It so happened that one of the workers was going to the port, and he offered to take Maria with him. The construction worker parked his vehicle in front of the port office and even introduced Maria to the office manager. This manager, when hearing Maria's request for a job, brought her to the office of the general manager. The general manager had Maria fill out an application, and then he interviewed her. Maria was hired right then as the new port accountant. She prayed, thanking God for the new job that she felt would help her accomplish her goal. Maria was grateful to the carpenter, but she never saw him again. When Maria thought of the people who had helped her, she was reminded of the Good Samaritan and Jesus.

Traditionalists who were born before 1946 are now considered legends. Then came the baby boomers, who were born from 1946 to 1964, and are the product of the sacrifices of the legends. Next come the generation Xers—born from 1965 to1979—who aggressively entered the arena.

The millennials, born from 1980 to 2000, came in recently with complexities. They dissected, evaluated, and quantified every move in order to balance their lives. Family, community, and environment were linked to their jobs. The competition and collaboration in the business arena contributed to behavior that was quite different from the generation Xers, baby boomers, and traditionalists. The millennials seemed to know it all.

My grandson, Angel, said to his mother one time, "Your eyes and your ears are the doorways to your mind and your heart. Be careful what you see and hear." Angel is a seven-year-old child. Sheltered millennial children seem to understand everything.

Yesterday I heard from Miracle, my five-year-old granddaughter. She said, "My thoughts come from my heart that grows and are connected to my spirit and brain. That is when I think best."

As I observed these children, I noticed also Erwin (four years old) dissecting and analyzing every meaning in a sentence.

There is more to learn and understand. These young children are sheltered with the love and values of their parents, coming from the previous generations who imparted their thoughts through books and stories, blended with the new technologies.

Years and years ago, the traditionalists timidly worked until retirement, the baby boomers worked their way up through hierarchy, and the generation Xers focused on the struggle to achieve work and life balance. Extensive communication also opened the mind of the millennial, as this generation was flooded with different ideas and perspectives. They observed cultural differences and similarities as they innovated, quantified, and pushed to create a difference in the world.

The creation of national business practices has increased the need for greater understanding of the problems and skills necessary for effective workers' personality differences, linked with one's unique experiences and related to national origin, culture, race, gender, and religion. This is common in globally diverse organizations.

Everyone is busy searching for strategy for balance or sometimes just moving with the flow of life. It doesn't matter if they are traditionalists, baby boomers, generation Xers, or millennials, or if they are at home or at work.

Chapter 2

The Foundation of Ethics

The Search for Meaning

Cultural diversity among ancient people has been inherited by the present generation. National and regional culture differences today still partly reflect the borders of the former empires. Eventually, history will involve a community characteristic that makes every cultural nation dependent on the past:

Culture	Country of Origin
Taoism	China
Buddhism	India
Hinduism	India
Judaism	Jew
Sikhism	Northern India
Zoroastrianism	Northeastern Iran
Shinto	Japan
Islam	Saudi Arabia
Confucius	China
Christianity	Palestine

The Foundation of Ethics

Taoism: Ethics and Individuals

"Make your heart like a lake. With a calm, still surface and great depths of kindness."
Lao Tzu

For over 2,500 years, the five thousand character of the Tao Te Ching was considered one of the greatest treasures in the world. Taoism is a religious tradition in China. The Tao Te Ching means "Classic of the Way and Virtue," (Chiang and Huang 2005). It is one of the most powerful of all Chinese philosophic and religious texts. It has spread outside the Far East and reaches as far as the West. The characters have multiple levels of interpretation, divided into two parts of eighty-one chapters apiece—from guidance on political leadership to instruction on higher spiritual development.

Taoism is all about experience. It deals with the nature, meaning, and practical implication of *Tao* and *Te*, two principles of supreme magnitude in Taoism. *Tao* was translated as "God, creation, nature, universal spirit and its look, or the way of all life." *Te* refers to "action, virtue, morality, beauty, and gracious behavior." The inner spirit of the Tao and Te has to be passed on through faithful commitment and practice which starts from the heart. Faith then follows. Our bodies are vessels that can glorify God through their destined journeys. Lao Tzu's teaching opens the heart and charges the willpower. Its universal power goes beyond cultural differences (Chiang and Huang 2005).

Buddhism: Ethics and Individuals

Our survival has depended and will continue to depend on our
basic goodness.
—Dalai Lama 1999

In India, the first sermon of the Buddha was preached. The Buddha
was born (a giant lotus provided a bed for him) in 556 BC in a small
village of Nepal, in the region of Tirai, Kapilavastu. He was the son of a
king of the tribe Shakya. He was named Prince Siddhartha. The refuge
(retreat) was composed of the Buddha (instructor), the Dharma (doctrine)
and the Sangha (community of monks) (Odier 1974).

An *ethical act* is said to be one that does not harm others' culture
and inner peace. Ethical behavior has a universal dimension, a potential
impact, and an assurance not to harm others. Ethics has always had a
connection with *spirituality*. This we can describe in terms of love,
compassion, patience, forgiveness, humility, and tolerance concerning
others' well-being.

How will we react to a genuine smile? One of the traits of a Buddhist is
a genuine smile—a natural humble act—one of the most beautiful values
a Buddhist can have. A smile can change one's direction and produce
love. Loving one another is a precious gift to everyone. Peace comes from
ethical behavior. Struggle comes to better our conduct. Compassion
connotes love, affection, kindness, gentleness, generosity of spirit, and
warm-heartedness (sympathy and kind words). The Buddhist thinks that
when he or she is kind to others, it creates peace in their own hearts and
in others' hearts as well. It also brings peace to family, to friends, to the
workplace, to the community, and so to the world. They believe that the

control of material well-being and knowledge is only a portion of what we need in life.

Buddhism fulfills short-term benefits for them and a long-term satisfaction for others. The spiritual actions they go through are because of others and make their lives meaningful. This is true happiness (Bstan-'dzin-rgya-mtsho 1999).

Hinduism: Ethics and Individuals

> We believe not only in universal toleration, but we accept all religions as true. I remember having repeated a hymn from my earliest boyhood, which is every day repeated by millions of human beings: "As the different streams having their sources in different places all mingle their water in the sea, so, O Lord, the different paths which men take through different tendencies, various though they appear, crooked or straight, all lead to Thee."
> —Swami Vivekananda's speech, The World Parliament of Religions: Chicago, September 11, 1893

Hinduism refers to any Indian religious tradition that is rooted in the earliest Indian religious books, called Vedas. These are composed of songs (chants and magic spells) and prayers that glorify different gods and goddesses. India has the god-king Rama, the humorous cowherd Krishna, and the divine mother Shakti who have all walked the earth and left behind blessings. And as Indians spread across Southeast Asia to Africa, and in more recent times to the West, faithful Hindus have brought the spirit of their religion with them and have endowed their new homes with it. What today is Hinduism is actually a system of religious and philosophical practices followed by various cultural and language groups throughout south Asia and wherever South Asians have migrated. By the end of the eighteenth century, English people (England) entered the Indian Territory. The Hindus were able to adopt the Western social and political concepts, while keeping their essential ideas and values.

Judaism: Ethics and Individuals

> It takes three things to attain a sense of significant being: God,
> a soul, and a moment.
> —Abraham J. Heschel, philosopher: 1927-1972

> The basis of Judaism is both faith and practice.
> —Herbert Tarr, *The Conversion of Chaplain Cohen*, 1963

Jewish gurus, regardless of their differences, are confident and have one belief that God has its supreme power. Like most of us, meditation is a portion of communing with God

The Jewish people, as interrelated with other cultures, civilization continuous. They are flexible and accept change, while their values are intact. Acceptance is always cheerful. Tradition also covered their culture, such as the celebration of *Purim* (emphasizing giving instead of taking) that commemorates the occasion on which Esther and Mordecai saved the Jews of Persia. *Yom Ha-atzma'ut* is a tradition they celebrate showing they care about one another, wherever they are. They were taught to have a responsibility to contribute to the community. The Hebrew Bible is the *Tanakh*, where you can read this story (Esther 9:22).

Sikhism: Ethics and Individuals

> Just as there is fragrance in the flower,
> And reflection in the mirror,
> Similarly, God lives within us;
> Search for Him in thy heart,
> O brother.
> —Introduction to Sikhism-Section V-Gubani (A.G. p. 684)

The background began in the Muslim-Hindu argument in the early sixteenth century in the state of Punjab in northern India. They believe in one God who can be found within. They call it the only guru that accentuated the unconditional unity and power, who created everything; and they are dependent on his will. They believe on living appropriately (*dharam khand*), deeper knowledge (*gian khand*), effort or joy (*saram khand*), and they believe that pride destroys the cleanness of the heart. The Sikh highly value community service (*seva*) (*Oxford Dictionary of World Religion*, 1997).

Zoroastrianism: Ethics and Individuals

> Active participation in life through good thoughts, good words, and good deeds is necessary to ensure happiness and to keep chaos at bay.
> —Zoroaster's concept of free will

Zoroaster was known in the West as the prophet of the religion. He lived in northeastern Iran in approximately 1200 BCE. He believed God (*Ahura Mazda*) anointed him through visions which were particularly centered on personal responsibility. Nigosian (1993) wrote that the Zoroastrian faith on God

(Ahura Mazda) and the Holy Spirit (Spenta Mainyu) is beyond measure. Zoroaster's teachings are based on good thoughts (*humata*), good deeds (*havarshta*), and good words (*hukhta*). Courage to practice the teachings showed progress on the spiritual path. Honesty is significant, and good actions include service. Their way of worship includes prayer

Shinto: Ethics and Individuals

> Purity is one of the fundamental virtues of Shinto ethics. Sincerity is also the guiding ethical principles of Shinto.
> (Sri Swami Sivananda 2005)

Besides Confucianism, Buddhism, and Taoism teaching, and some Christian influence, Shinto is one among the source of the beliefs and practices of the indigenous in Japan. Shinto was introduced in the sixth century CE.

> Shinto emphasizes gratitude to the *kami* (God) and to the ancestors, from whom life and all the blessings come. The purpose of the Shinto is to realize and carry out the will of the *kami* and the ancestors in the family, the community, and the nation. Humans, like the whole of nature, are children of the *kami*. They are therefore, inherently good and need only to have their defilement removed for the natural goodness to shine through. (John Bowker 1997)

Islam: Ethics and Individuals

> Righteous is he who believes in Allah of the last day and the
> angels and the scriptures and the prophets.
> (Qur'an 2:177)

Eid al-Fitr is a Muslim occasion at the end of Ramadan. Prayer is their way to communicate to Allah. The prophet Muhammad, the first leader in Arabian society, praised diversity. The Qur'an teaches Muslims to be kind, spiritual, family oriented, and devout.

Christianity: Ethics and Individuals

> But seek ye first the kingdom of God, and his righteousness;
> and all these things shall be added unto you.
> (Matthew 6:33 KJV)

> Therefore if thine enemy hunger, feed him, if he thirst,
> give him drink; for in so doing thou shalt heap coals of
> fire on his head.
> (Romans 12:20 KJV)

> Recompense to no man evil for evil. Provide things
> honest in the sight of all men. If it be possible, as much
> as lieth in you, live peaceably with all men.
> (Romans 12:17-18 KJV)

Christians have different values and beliefs. Christians believe a book called The Holy Bible as their basis of Christianity. They also have a variety of interpretations of the Bible. Most if not all believe that Jesus is the Lord and Savior. Thus, the teaching of Jesus molds the heart of Christians.

In addition, one's faith begins from the heart as it believes God's Word. While a nation's culture and tradition have a strong hold on everyone in the community, the refinement of life depends on having peace with God through Jesus Christ. Keeping God's Word and practicing it in one's daily life, and allowing the fruit of the Holy Spirit to develop is a long nurturing of self—heart, mind, and spirit. The human inner conflict is between the indwelling Spirit of God and the unquenchable ego (self), between surrender to the power of self and the full display of power of God in the heart, mind, and spirit.

Spiritual Relationship

The teachings of religions and philosophers are called *dogma* (or concepts). Basically, this is an ingredient to culture. Cultural diversity is common to the present market which changes the normal way of being in the workplace. Common to all is the emphasis on the faith to our Creator; the compassion, kindness, gentleness, patience, humbleness, and unity to everyone.

Respect then is one of the keys to realization of the millennials' dream: unity. Since everyone has one belief, why then do we squabble? How do we differ? As we always talk of complexities, Huntington (1996) wrote that the primary tension of the twenty-first century is the "conflicts based on religion, from the West." Whereas, Guy (2000) mentioned that during the Cold War, the Eastern World had the concept often seen in the Far East—a region that tolerates significant cultural and religious harmony, Eastern philosophy, art, literature, and other traditions including Buddhism and Hindu Yoga.

Where then do our morals meet? How will we crush the differences? How complicated is it to be united, and how do we accomplish this?

How do we blend religion, politics, culture, technology, finance, national security, and ecology, and eliminate or shrink the traditional boundaries? These are questions we didn't even want to think about. In summary, how will we shape our lives? What balance are we looking for? How strong is our faith? Here is the definition of faith as written in Hebrews 11:1: "Now faith is the substance of things hoped for, the evidence of things not seen." And according to the teaching of Buddhism, "Faith is a facet of which is recognition of some term of supernatural reality, including perhaps an idea of heaven or nirvana." As we read further, we will encounter simple stories and experiences that will answer the issue.

Chapter 3

Bridging the Gap from West to East

Our beliefs and abilities can make a positive difference each day. Benjamin Franklin[3] earned the title of "The First American" for his early and untiring demonstration for colonial unity. He was considered to be one of the greatest American minds. Franklin stated that intelligence, passion, strength, devotion, charisma, tenacity, perseverance, generosity, and forgiveness makes a good leader.

From the Australian point of view, Mark Vaile, Australian Minister for Trade, said in his speech, "Australia and India; Business and the Bilateral relationship," (New Delhi, October 16, 2000), that businesspeople must be trained in the areas of patience, perseverance, and persistence.

Socrates, known as one of the founders of Western philosophy,[4] in his simple ways practiced perseverance, patience, and persistence as a measurement of ethics. In their own way, philosophers and business people practice and apply these same characteristics in their daily routine.

Records show that some of the West's greatest leaders have been praying people. This was confirmed when British Prime Minister Tony

---

[3]   1706-1790

[4]   469-399 BC

Blair stated he would be judged on the Iraq war by "my Maker," (Chris Armstrong; May 30, 2003). Many more were named in the past, and one of them was France's Louis IX (1214-1270) who was well known for his faith and accomplishments. He was a servant leader with exceptional humility and perseverance, and for this reason cannot be considered a hypocrite.

China, known to be ancient, had Confucius (551-479 BC), a moral teacher who witnessed the beginning of Taoism, Buddhism, and Greek philosophy. He believed in the power of faith and that respectfulness, tolerance, honesty, meticulous intelligence, and kindness were learned behaviors—he called this *wisdom*.

Florida V. Ortiz (2003) in her manifesto, "Priority Problems & Questions on the State & Traditions of Filipino Philosophy," pointed out Dr. Jose P. Rizal, a model leader of Philippine history, emphasized, *"Ang di marunong lumingon sa pinanggalingan; Di makakarating sa paroroonan,"* ("Gratitude is an ingredient to reaching your goal."). The Filipino leader philosophy indicated the relationship of humility and gratitude. It may be an excerpt we can connect to a Scripture before 2000 BC: "The fear of the Lord is the instruction of wisdom; and before honour is humility" (Proverbs 15:33 KJV). Up to this point, the current practice of moral virtue has connections from the past. It seems old-fashioned to some, but to those searching for spiritual autonomy supported with a blend of ideologies, they may consider linking the past to the current moral values. From this quote, we may also look upon the blending of different cultures, geographical locations, and more differences which serve as a challenge to everyone's leadership.

Effective or Efficient?

We are now leaning on a new set-up of management where managers are also leaders. How would this complexity work? Let us blend these two personalities. The "manager does the things right, while the leader does the right things" (Drucker 2006). Managers are efficient, and leaders are effective. The focus of these two roles is on the strengths, weaknesses, and potentials of the workforce. We preach the role of thoughts and then practice those concepts in our life. I have heard many times: "Practice what you preached." But most of the time, it is easier to preach than to actually practice what was preached. Most people just say, "Walk the talk." Businesses most often identify leaders with "soft skills" as those who have the ability to bring projects to successful conclusions, and those with the "hard skills" who have a common set of goals and procedures. There should also be mutual respect, open communications, and openness to new ideas and thinking, and since this is the workforce of millennials, leadership always intertwines with management.

Although managers grew up in a particular society in a particular period, and their ideas cannot help but reflect the constraints of their environment, the challenge is to integrate the practice of "management and leadership" in a domestic or international business. To see how the game is changing, let's look back on the sixteenth century, when Michel de Montaigne, a Frenchmen, wrote a statement which was made famous by Blaise Pascal about a century later:

> "*Verite en-deca-des Pyrennes, erreur, au-dela*": There are truths
> on this side of the Pyrenees that are falsehoods on the other.

While Michel de Montaigne emphasized the difference of culture in society, we can consider looking further. Soon we will learn to appreciate other cultures and to incorporate the differences with those of our neighboring nations.

In a survey conducted with North American and Filipino managers in 2007, it was noted that the strategies were identified as "emotional intelligence." As it has been defined by Daniel Goleman (1995), self-awareness, self-management, social awareness, and social skills were critical indicators in life. These were shaped by childhood experience and could be improved and developed throughout life. The survey was given to lower and middle managers whose answers were based on their experiences from their childhood, home, community, and workplace. Before then, researchers believed that emotion was a vital stimulant for ethical values such as trust, integrity, empathy, resilience, and credibility which are advantageous to maintaining business relationships (Gardner 1993; Fukuyuma 1995; Whitney 1996; Drucker 1999; Bass 1995). This view was so popular that it spread around the world from the West to the East. Looking back, Immanuel Kant (1724-1804) argued that experience is purely subjective.

> The result of the survey showed that there was a significant difference between the two cultures. The emotional intelligence of the American sample had a positive correlation with the effectiveness in a new business environment, whereas the emotional intelligence of the Filipino sample showed an inverse correlation with the effectiveness in a new business environment. The Filipino sample based from the survey data suggested that as age or education increases, the new business effectiveness decreases. The American sample suggested that as education increases, business effectiveness increases.[5]

---

[5]   Result based on the point-biserial correlation statistic.

Like the observation of Michel de Montaigne in his country and neighboring countries, the participants in the survey of the United States and the Philippines have their differences too. What will we do to take care of the differences? How far in our level of ethics or values shall we go to construct diverse cultures that are workable in the workplace?

While the spiritual leaders nurture love, joy, peace, long suffering, gentleness, goodness, faith, meekness, and temperance (Galatians 6:22-23), leaders of different generations and cultures (like Socrates, Jose P. Rizal, Benjamin Franklin, Mark Vaile, and Tony Blair) have told us that when intelligence, passion, charisma, generosity, forgiveness, perseverance, patience, faith, humility, respectfulness, honesty, tolerance, wisdom, and kindness are practiced, this indicates a high moral value. This can construct diverse cultures that are workable in the workplace.

Entrepreneurship

A manager acted more of a leader in an entrepreneurial business. The traditionalist, baby boomers, generation Xers seemed to be convinced to join the millennials in their way of doing business. Besides financial capital, these traders find understanding, commitment, courage, integrity, and global marketing should be added to the process. Entrepreneurs worked one day at a time to accomplish their goals. Instead of following a written business plan, they assume the process of running a business is in their mind. Entrepreneurs persevere with their team. Everyone seems to be hardworking, honest, and patient. Furthermore, through faithful commitment, the entrepreneurs respect cultural differences. They worked together with trust. Their teams make time to pray together for a work well done, and to reach the business goal and their personal goals as well.

Chapter 4

Historic Enhancement

As we walk further, we notice that social and motivational differences are groups to work around the world and across nations, states, and regions of diverse people and cultures. Understanding and respecting one's culture motivates positive results to anyone. Since religion affects behavior in a region, it is always appropriate to intensely consider adding the concept to the agenda.

How then will the historical principles and modern-day techniques blend?

As I went through the process of landing a job in the past, the hiring management staff gave random IQ[6] tests. They hired those with the highest score, since the intellectual people always use IQ to evaluate the ability of an individual. EQ,[7] which was brought up and had been a cover story of *Time* magazine on October 2, 1995, came to existence to quantify one's emotional value. This rating of emotional value in our daily life and in the business world was widely accepted. Since intelligence and emotions can be tested, then it is rational to suggest that spiritual value could also be added and quantified. Eventually, to produce the effective

---

6   IQ: Intellectual quotient
7   EQ: Emotional quotient

and efficient leader will hiring staff be looking for an equal ratio of 1:1:1, or the average proportion of what would be about a 50/50 split between cognitive, emotional, and spiritual compatibility?

Table 1: Will this ratio balance your life?
Is this effective for every individual?

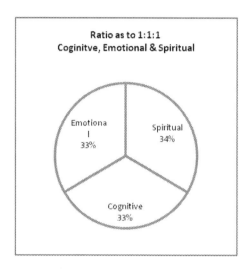

Furthermore, everyone is born with a heart and brain. According to psychologists and researchers[8] there is a part of the brain, the amygdala, that is responsible for our emotional and social responses and memories. The amygdala is connected with the mental and emotional condition of a person, and it is located a few inches away from both ears. *Amygdala* is the Greek word for "almond," and the amygdala has the size and appearance of an almond.[9] While the heart is emotional, the brain has its mental power. Although emotions come and go, our spiritual value is there to stay. As we grow up, through the nurturing of our parents and through mingling with our surroundings, the function of our heart and brain flourish. Thus,

---

8   From 1888

9   Priya Johnson published by Google, 15 July 2010. Retrieved, 19 April 2011.

our "mind, emotion, and spirit" start from childhood and flourishes as we grow older.

Then, how much of these values do we need to balance our way of life? Will culture intervene in our growth to learn?

Those working either for domestic or global organizations or businesses also desire to be effective leaders. Hypothetically, the ratio of 1:1:1 may not apply to every individual. There will be differences, according to how we were raised by our parents, and our relationship with the society and what environment we are in.

Illustrations below show different proportion where an individual's capability may fit in to balance life. Although the table shows these proportions, every individual has its own proportion of balancing his life.

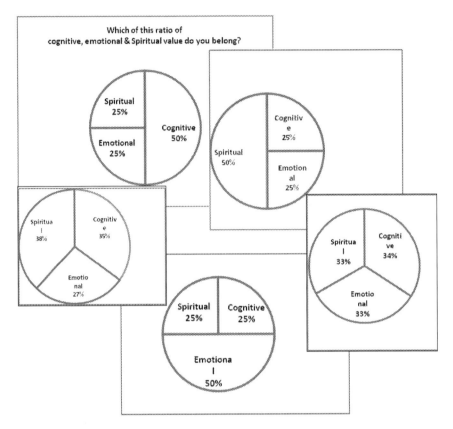

Table 2: Which of this ratio works for you?
Or, is there another ratio that fits you?

Creativity and Production

As we move forward, business creativeness blends the past and the present to produce. Much has changed in recent years, from simple things that our forefathers taught us to the many complexities that we learn as time goes by. Let us walk to the side of the workers. In the past, applicants found job vacancies in newspapers and sometimes through people passing information to one another. Currently, more options have been added. The present job seekers through the click of a mouse can find job listings in the Internet. Now applicants are free to surf for jobs anywhere in the world. Employers in one way or the other, hope for applicants' honesty.

Some companies rely on computer programs to evaluate resumes. Applicants on the other side, send well-written résumés to prove themselves capable of the job. For the balance of the equation, the integrity of an applicant is quantified through an interview or a simple survey questions. But some human resource people still believe in the format of past résumés which show the details of the employment history. Applicants also hope for interviews and pray that the interviewer can read between the lines to see their hidden wisdom.

From this point, experience, values, and academic credential are quantified. Résumés are concise. A single-page résumé is best, but others consider two pages. Some firms interview applicants via satellite, thinking every applicant will give them the answer as expected. Thus, the applicants hope the recruiter can read between the lines and that they will notice the body language or any hidden values of those being interviewed.

While jobs are reachable, music composers tried to blend different melodies. Frank Zappa[10] of Baltimore, Maryland, an iconic guitarist, fashionable composer, and innovative record producer, put together rock, jazz, and added orchestral music in a span of four decades. It became popular in the market, and old songs came back to business. As we all listen to music, classic, instrumental, pop, or rock, and old songs have become hits.

Hundreds of innovators tried something new. And the current education also gets a piece of the pie. Schools went global and embraced macrolearning, having the idea that employers needed flexible workers.

---

[10]   1940-1993

Everything is moving fast. Schools affiliate with other schools across borders. Speaking two languages is a norm.

Most if not all beckoned to reinvasion the way we organize our lives to the community and environment. Socrates (469-399 BC) is known for his irresistible passion communicating with people—young or old, poor or rich. Not only was Socrates humble, his ideas regarding ethics were exceptional. As Strathern, (1997) wrote, rather than questioning the world, Socrates believed we should first know ourselves. He adopted the celebrated maxim, *"Gnothi seauton"*—"know thyself."

The Best of the Millennial

Plato witnessed Socrates's principles of ethics. Socrates insisted that true ethics is a way of life committed to high moral character showing wisdom that comes from the Creator (Navia 2007). Plato was a student of Socrates. Aristotle was a student of Plato. Plato was the first to blend everything that we try to blend in life today, like religion, economics, art, psychology, history, science, math, politics, literature, and love (Cavalier 1990). Moreover, Aristotle (384-322 BC) discovered modern science. Aristotle divided the activity of men into two aspects—moral (truth and goodness), and social being (work well done).

More so, the intellect of the East speaks of experience that deals with nature (which includes God), creation, universal spirit, virtue, morality, beauty, and gracious behavior. These are the ideas of the past philosophers. In addition, the works of historians, poets, religious leaders, and authors encourages and inspires the millennials.

Followed them was Immanuel Kant,[11] one of the greatest thinkers of all time. Kant focused his writing on individual morality and social responsibility. Kant mentioned that "one cannot fail to expect that many similarities to the ideas of the past can be found for every new idea discovered."

Furthermore, despite of the popularity of Yahoo and Google, millennials also showed interest in the past. Millennials, like traditionalists, baby boomers, and generation Xers, love to read newspapers and magazines circulating in all parts of the world. Let us go to a scene that occurs in a passenger airplane where something caught my eye.

Before we got in the plane, a newspaper was offered to us. In front of our seat was a magazine written specifically about the activities and destination of the air carrier. This may be a sort of advertisement, and at the same time provided entertainment to the passengers. It seems that marketing not only is busy on land, but also in the air.

The stewardess was also busy selling different products to passengers. The flyers in this case were treated equally—traditionalists, baby boomers, generation Xers, and millennials were all looking for a possible future trip, while scrutinizing the products. It is breathtaking to see these groups thinking the same way with all the gadgets the millennials acquired and offered.

Wonders in the East

Reengineering, restructuring, and downsizing are resulting in a world in which outsourcing of all brand-related activities has become the norm. While managers become less controlling, leaders nurture a social

---

[11]   1724-1804

community of workers that encourages confident people to work together to exercise their own creativity. Leaders developed the capacity for personal leadership stemming from a deep self-awareness that builds up from the inside out rather than the outside in.

I was in Beijing before the Olympics in 2007, and I noticed the speed of the demolition and construction of buildings around the area where the Olympic buildings were constructed. It was a fast decision, showing leadership and firmness. It went on and on and not a single complaint was heard from anyone. Although the construction was going on, the Great Wall of China, the Forbidden City, and the Summer Palace showed how the pride of the past was being preserved for people of the world to see. Simple trading was common at the foot of the Great Wall. The trade blended the past and the present generations.

Two days later I was in Shanghai. It was an hour or two before darkness would set in, and the neon lights started twinkling all over. I was at McDonalds and ordered a drink. I looked around and noticed the big buildings. Then I thought about the pictures I had seen in magazines. One in my group noticed me, and said it was like Paris. Yes, I think that was the picture that I was trying to draw in my mind. Shanghai is a modern city by itself.

I remember when the British handed over Hong Kong to Chinese control (1997); some Hong Kong residents migrated to Vancouver, Canada. And the simple trade flooded Vancouver.

Hope and Culture

It was the summer of 2010, and I was enjoying my stay in Hawaii. Last night I was invited to attend a seminar with a group of ladies of different cultures—native Hawaiians; Micronesians (Kosraean, Palauan, Ponapean, and Chamorro); Asians (Chinese, Japanese, Koreans, Filipinos, Vietnamese, and Thais); Samoans; Puerto Ricans; Australians; Caucasians; and Blacks, to name a few.

The emcee handled a lively introduction. She made everybody laughed at her jokes and quizzes. The speaker came from mainland United States, and the tone of the topic was from the outside, and the participants were diverse, coming from the West and East. To the local participant, they were all new to the experience relayed. But as each related the circumstance to her experience, it seemed that what they had outside Hawaii was correlated to what they had achieved. This very clear message made the participants dream how wonderful it was to hear others' experiences and how those could be related to their own experiences. As I noticed the happiness in them; I thought it was a challenge to managers to listen to the experiences of simple people to encourage them to be receptive to the diverse workforce.

The theory of Mary Parker Follet (1868-1933), recognized as a prophet of management, blended together what she learned from a small group, called a team, in an organization and society believing that through teamwork, management and workers could work hand in hand for the benefit of the organization and society. Follet also introduced empowerment to every workforce—the concept having been copied from community associations. The management concept of Mary Parker Follet was implemented in some businesses in Japan. The philosophy was about developing the character or emotional values of the workforce. Business found the perception advantageous to the organization, the workers, and the community as well. Practicing the Mary Parker Follet concept, the Japanese industries flourished.

A month later, I attended a ladies group meeting. I noticed the speaker and participants were of the same ethnic group. Although they differed in age, the glow in their eyes showed they were happy and comfortable. The meeting ended in a few hours. But the socializing lasted for few more hours. This was a good start to open a participant to a wider horizon.

In December 2010, I attended a ladies' monthly meeting in Oak Harbor. The participants were Caucasians and Filipinos of the same organization. They called it a "refreshing" meeting. The group exchanged views of life demonstrating what they had done in the past month and their goals for the following month. Whatever the speaker wanted to bring out in her message, the participants seemed happy they were there. Everyone seemed contented. Everybody participated in the discussion, and after the meeting was refreshment and socializing. The group graciously thanked God for the good things that happened in their lives.

I visited Chinatown in Hawaii. Like Hong Kong or other countries in Asia, there are small traders—mostly Asians—like Filipinos, Chinese, Koreans, and Japanese. I noticed that most of these people, besides making profits, are happy communicating to people and showing their heritage.

Most people enjoy preserving their own culture. The modern world introduces yoga, bhangra music, curry, barbecue, adobo—these represent just a few of the ways that activities and foods are also integrated. I was in Seoul early this year, and I found myself eating Thai food. The Thai food that I ate was similar to *sinigang* to Filipinos with the difference being the color of the food that was added. While people migrated and discovered new delicacies, everything is now accessible on the Internet. For example, "barbecue" in Western culture and "broil" in Eastern culture both refer to grilled foods.

Focusing on the Present Trade

The World Trade Organization joined the two large countries of the United States and China in the world of business (WTO News: 2001 Press releases, Press/243, 17 September 2001). Although both are almost the same geographically (area), there are differences in the way business operates in each country. But the differences did not bother the manufacturing businesses and foreign investors when they took a big risk by moving to China. Unexpectedly, these businesses gave their customers systematic rethinking. In the old days, the common belief was that imported products from United States were beyond compare. Now, many products are made in China by United States businesses. It is puzzling how customers accepted the big change. Much to the surprise of all, it was accepted so fast that more firms followed. Because wages are low and the prices of commodities are low, joint leadership was also accepted. Thus, the result was functional. After all, collaboration of leaders across nations is accepted in the community.

Motor vehicles seem to be very popular these days. Every nation is contributing to the trade. It looks like every car model of different car manufacturing firms follow the same pattern. With the difference of the manufacturer's name and quality control brand name, integration and collaboration is manifested to the industry.

I attend leadership meetings, seminars, and workshops with small and big groups. I always enjoy listening to different speakers. I noticed that although the speakers discuss the same topic, the thought differs. I observed that the culture of the speaker makes the difference. I notice also that every speaker discusses an idea stating his own perception. Combining all these perceptions, a listener can differentiate between both sides of the fence and can form a rational design. For example, various speakers who create different thoughts and perceptions regarding environment and society craft this diverse explanation: the difference in perception doesn't strangle creativity. Instead, they are seen as a way to channel creativity into a new form of leadership. At first, it may seem awkward and time consuming, but the extra time listening to them will pay off. Finally, shared leadership across a team of leaders is excellent to global industries.

Furthermore, effective leaders are fast to grasp particular strengths and weaknesses of others. These leaders persevere and become compassionate, patient, and humble as they understand, listen, and reach out to the workforce. Establishments continue to thrive as leaders continue to offer their unique experience. However, we seldom offer ourselves simple honest opinion, like understanding others the way we understand ourselves. Most of the time, complexity comes our way and that's when our mind starts waggling.

How could the culture of a business in a mother company be carried to our subsidiary company? Let me walk you through a merged organization. It is a practice of most merged organizations to share management. In the process, tension remains in the two companies on joint meetings. It seems that whatever decision is made, someone does not like it. Although both sides understand, the success of the project depends on the joint decision of the two groups. Complexity does not allow them to understand that decision is best for those who will use it. Respect for one another and collaboration are always required to reach goals.

In another example, there were two foreign businesses that put up a joint venture in Palau. They funded a promising "services" business. The business flourished for a while, and then suddenly collapsed. We might call this mismanagement. Mismanagement is not always the reason for decreasing business. In this case, others blamed it on foreign policies. Most said it was lack of financial resources. However, mistakes, like the failure of most businesses come from the shortage of research or sometimes from management's lack of integrity. Thinking of research, business owners might as well add in the research observation, evaluation, and analysis of operation of both small and big businesses in that particular area. For the ongoing study, more space to culture and moral values of the workforce should be prioritized. This way, multinationals (corporations, enterprises, and organizations) and entrepreneurial businesses will continue to flourish without disruption.

However, out of all these missed processes, a manager's aim is to be aware of one country's culture and at the same time be aware of the workers' strengths and weaknesses. This way, leaders may heed to simple and honest communication. Compassionate and patient leaders aware of a diverse workforce understand every perception the workers may offer to the organization.

In one instance, a leader of a foreign business and a leader of a local business both directed one joint venture project. The business owners had a mutual agreement to jointly manage the project. The two agreed to put up a hotel business in which the foreign business partner agreed to build the hotel in the land of the local partner. Both agreed to divide the profit equally. As soon as the operation started, the relationship became sour. The local partner disregarded the agreement and took over the management. In this particular scenario, what was missing was compassion and understanding.

We are all looking for a change. Which of these will work? Which will not? Leaders say, "Do the right thing." How? The solution might be as simple as saying "respect." Let us look at what "respect" means to each one.

Kevin Rollins, president and COO, and Michael Dell, chairman and CEO (2003) are a good combination of leaders. The two top management people of Dell Computer with their collaborating strategy marketed their products without difficulties. The top management people added company ethics and standards as a way of improving morale to the workforce. The company culture was "We Got Wealthy," and to be a great company, Dell added, "We've got a long way to go."[12] The success started from the humbleness of the leaders and was passed down to the entire workforce.

---

[12] Time Global Business; Cathy Booth Thomas, July 28, 2003.

Chapter 5

Leaders outside Their Comfort Zone

Traditional Approaches and Global Leadership

Organization leaders of multiregional locations across same-nation states or across borders are "global" leaders. Countries have a huge variety of leadership styles, partly produced by historical, cultural, and regulatory differences. For consideration, flexibility and the ability to refrain from labeling others' perspective as "right" or "wrong" can be the key skill of the global leader. Each culture, company, or individual brings a unique communication style and work ethic. Global competition imposes higher global standards of customer service, creativity, and innovation that even companies with no global ambitions are forced to meet to protect their market shares. Decision making varies from person to person, from organization to organization, and from culture to culture, according to the configuration of the business. Everything cannot be standardized. Let us have a glance at an episode in a medical clinic that happened in a small country.

A woman who was injured at work visited her family physician. After an hour of waiting, in walked a woman she had just met. The woman started talking: "Your finger is normal for old people like you. You are older than me, and my finger has the same problem as yours. What was your work?" And she answered her own question. "A cashier?" The patient answered, "My finger was hurt because of an injury." The lady continued, "That is normal for older people." The patient was persistent, maybe because of the pain. Since the woman didn't respond to the objections of the patient, the patient slowly walked out. The woman followed her outside. Eventually the patient, with a low voice, asked, "What is your name?" And the lady with a high tone said, "I am Jean, a nurse." That ended the dialogue. The patient walked away humbly and didn't say a word. The conversation ended up on a sour note on the part of the customer. How many more people like Jean will a customer encounter? What would happen if Jean had taken care of the customer?

In a past generation, with indigenous people, there was an episode that could be treasured even these days. Let us read a scenario that happened during World War II in the island of Luzon, Philippines.

A soldier who was really humble and sensitive to the needs of indigenous people, called *Aeta* or *Negrito*, was in the death march in WWII. Before that happened, the soldier visited the Aetas in the mountains, bringing them malaria medicine. Malaria, which was common in their village, caused numerous deaths in the community. Besides the medicine, this man always remembered to bring canned goods that were foreign to the villagers. These people usually lived in the mountains of Zambales, Philippines. When the Japanese occupied the island in WWII, the soldier was one of those in the death march to Capas, Bataan. There was no hope for these people to live. In the middle of the night, the indigenous people took the chance to help the soldier by pulling him away from the group. They brought the soldier to a nearby river and laid him there for the whole night while they waited for the line of people in the death march to pass. The Aetas brought the soldier to their village and took care of him until he was able to get to his feet. The scenario showed that in any situation, whatever culture people are, love plays a royal role in various ways. Any time and in any situation, love always finds ways to help.

We sometimes depend on technology for every success, although in every instance, decisions still depend on the leader. Business and organizations are also dependent on the leaders' decisions. May I walk you through this episode:

A US Airways plane was almost at its destination when birds hit the engine and disabled the plane. The pilot, Chesley B. Sullenberger, after consulting with aviation officials and experts, made a quick decision and crash-landed the plane into the Hudson River, New York. Many of the passengers called on God; they repented and prayed. The decision of the pilot was amazing to everybody.[13] The landing was safe and all the passengers were safe as well.

Flexibility, Collaboration, and Competition

August of 2010, my son invited me to his place in Honolulu, Hawaii. A week after I landed in Honolulu, we went shopping at COSTCO, a wholesale chain store. In the cashier section, I had been observing how two baggers interacted in their work. They worked this way:

One bagger unloaded our groceries. While waiting for the cashier to start ringing up groceries, he went to the adjacent cash register and helped bag the goods for another customer. While working with the other cash register operator, the cashier on our side started ringing up our groceries.

---

[13] FacebookTwitterDiggdeliclousredditMySpaceStumbleUponLinkedin; January 15, 2009.

The other bagger near us started putting our groceries in bags. It was a harmonious collaboration of workers. And this is exceptional.

I remember what Daniel Goleman (2005), wrote in his book:

> A mistake will be prevented if a group worked together harmoniously. Teamwork, open lines of communication, cooperation, listening, and speaking one's mind. (p. 148)

This episode is a challenge to the leadership of an organization. The great challenge to leaders is how they gain knowledge and real understanding in a wide variety of geographical areas and how they build and articulate a clear vision, even as both the workforce and clientele become increasingly diverse. At the same time, most multileveled organizational structures present barriers to communication.

I visited China in 2007. From Hong Kong, Kowloon, Beijing, Shanghai, Wuhan, and Guangzhou, I traveled through a railroad carrier and a ferryboat to Macao. I stayed two nights in every place, except in Macao where I spent one day. We left Kowloon in the daytime and arrived in Beijing the following day.

While in the train, everybody seemed to be friends. I had a chance to listen to a Chinese and a Filipino youngster—both may have been kindergarten age. They acted as if they knew each other. They seemed to understand each other, because they were giggling while playing. The boys separated only when it was time to take a nap. It was a wonder to see them that way, because the Filipino child spoke Tagalog, and the Chinese child spoke Mandarin. They played, they giggled, they tumbled. At that moment, I imagined if only we could be like them. We might be able to build a pleasant relationship.

I noticed a girl at her teens smiling at me, and I returned her smile. In a few seconds, we were talking. The locomotive was so slow, that in the time it took to get to Beijing, we felt as if we had known each other for a long time. The smiles and laughter between us opened a good communication. Although I opened a Mandarin pamphlet to translate my message, we felt comfortable to one another. The transparency of the conversation made us build a friendship.

I was in a hotel in Shanghai. A receptionist there smiled openly, when I bowed and said, "*Ni hao*" (hello). I said, "I'm foreign to your country and eager to learn your language." And she answered me, "*Ni hao.*" In return I said, "*Xie-xie*" (thank you). Hoping that I was right, the lady smiled and slowly started speaking in English. Through this observation, I believed that even in language, countries are integrated. We both laughed at the situation. After the event, I felt comfortable and enjoyed my stay in the hotel.

I dined in a restaurant in Shanghai, and gave a five dollar (US) tip. Timidly she gave back the money and politely told me that I had paid more than the cost of the food I ate. Because I was satisfied with the service, I said, "The five dollars are for you." But still the waitress insistently gave it back. Thus, different countries not only have diverse cultures but also have different perceptions in life. Patience, understanding, and respecting the differences, make one happy and comfortable.

While cognitive ability is very important in the business arena—like math, reading, and writing—there are other abilities and beliefs that are equally critical to learn to stay competitive. Moral values combined with cognitive ability always intertwine for the effectiveness of a business leader. Thus, moral value is an important ability that should be added to everyone's advantage. Currently, teams are becoming popular in the business arena. But for some time, newly hired workers and lower ranking workers were treated differently.

For instance, in a small cafeteria, a newly hired custodian was assigned to work with two supervisors. Both supervisors gave orders to this worker. And after work, the world was spinning around to the new worker and she ended up with a headache. She tried to comply with the instructions of the two supervisors. In this case, floor supervisors should also be briefed regarding duties of a new worker.

A scenario in a fast-food restaurant paralleled the above scenario: A waiter picked up a piece of paper on the floor near the table of a customer. The waiter put the paper on the customer's table, thinking the customer owned the paper. The waiter was happy, thinking he had helped the customer. But the customer, with an angry gesture, called the waiter over and scolded him for the paper he left on their table, considering it trash. The waiter was stunned and accepted the blame, then moved on. Misunderstanding is not only on lower ranks of workers, but can also happen in the higher ranks. Thus, customer service training at all levels should be put into practice. The waiter had honest intentions by placing the piece of paper on the customer's table. The customer, misunderstanding the waiter's intention, reacted. Sometimes this circumstance is nothing to business owners, but most of the time it causes a worker to be laid off and might also be a basis for damage to the reputation of a business.

Who is to take charge with the situation like the above? How will the workers have more understanding of situations and at the same time, be sensitive to the attitude of others and maintain a pleasant work environment?

Accompanied by the spin of spiritual, religious, and moral choices that exist among different believers, traditionalists, baby boomers, generation Xers, and millennials in their own ways, share common values in creating solutions that often make them similar to one another: they commune with God. Other than this, peers are always around to judge relationships and society. Let us examine another scenario:

A flight attendant took a child from her mother after the woman slapped the crying child for kicking her. The other passengers asked the question, Does the flight attendant have the right to mediate, since our society dictates that we are not to mind others' business? Everyone has the ability to understand our own emotions and develop self-discipline. This is remarkable, because the flight attendant was able to work with the mother of the child. The flight attendant, with her love, used her wisdom, judgment, and understanding. On her own evaluation of the situation, and according to appropriate values she had, she needed to help the mother and her child.[14]

---

[14]   Leanne Italie and Sue Major Holmes; Associated Press Writers, August 19, 2010

Chapter 6

In Search of Reason

Taking from the past, the true measure of leadership depends on the practice of ethics. A current example of this is carrying out less glamorous roles that coaches know are vital to team success. Besides the business goal, individuals also have goals, needs, and dreams that must be cared for. This is challenging and most critical to discuss in a team. Blending the company's and each individual's goal is what leadership is all about. Let me walk you to a scenario where workers came from different backgrounds, had different goals and dreams, and were blessed with unique skills.

This scenario happened in one of the restaurants in Malakal, Palau. The business operation of the restaurant with stable customers got the attention of the management. Besides the restaurant's one hundred and more possible customers taking breakfast, coffee, and dinner, there were customers who ate in the restaurant while working on any business transaction they had to do in the port. Thus, a secured income from the employees was already in the box. Lunch was not countable since most had a *bento* (lunch box). We can consider the other customers as additional income. As implied, the restaurant was not making any profit. The mission: to turn around the operation from loss to gain. Do we need to toss a coin to make this happen?

Listening and thinking vividly, I realized the cognitive ability is not sufficient to grip the circumstance. Not only was the workforce culturally diverse, but also it differed in their working values. Most probably, more meticulous effort had to be shaped to complete the work. Looking back from the ancient times "When those leaders strived to achieve a goal; the hunger, fatigue, or discomfort experience hardly bothered them. In addition, the leaders played as mentors; compassionate and committed to support their group." As I think farther, I considered that copying this process would work with this group. Thus, the collaboration of the cognitive, emotional, and spiritual compatibility will again work. Who will benefit and who will not?

After the introduction, the manager explained that the company expected an "effective fruitful result." Our first day was full of fun as we got to know each other personally, and we defined everyone's line of duties. A trust was built between us. Communication within the group became smooth. Suggestions and contributions of ideas were open and accepted. Everyone was committed to the goal: "an effective fruitful result." Everyone in the group focused on future possibilities. Mentoring was satisfying. After the meeting, a change was displayed in the workplace. While information circulated, the organizational procedure and employee behavior slowly moved in the expected direction and the potential within started to grow. Eventually the group started working as a team.

From day one to the last day working with the group, a harmonious environment, a developed trust, and a workable communication was nurtured. Motivating one another with an open heart was observed; a full change was implemented. A month after, the workforce showed a total change in their working values. Everyone was committed to their work. The organizational structure and procedure ran smoothly. Employee behavior deserted self and learned to serve. The process ran strategically smooth. The cash flow did not run dry. Finally, the restaurant accumulated profit. As a result, the management earned more than they expected. Not only that, the workforce was totally changed. They were empowered, committed, and trusted employees. Eventually the management gave the workers a pay raise and benefits. Both the management and the workforce reached their goal. Cognitive ability and emotional competence linked with spiritual strength intertwined in the workforce. Thus, it was a win-win situation to those involved: the workforce, the management, and the community they served.

Chapter 7

Accepting Diversity

It is a daily routine to say that we live in a period of extraordinary change. The traditionalists, baby boomers, and generation Xers are watching or sometimes marching with the millennials.

In more than a decade, a large number of changes were made. Border barriers were minimized or eliminated. Businesses became flexible and vulnerable to all issues. Not surprisingly, many nations tried to survive the flow, while people squabbled. Infrastructures continue to rise, overseas jobs become challenging. Employers continue to retrain employees. Entrepreneurs blossom like mushrooms. An increasing competition from region to region jeopardizes social stability. Collaboration increased competition. Educational opportunities sprouted throughout, as if travel from East to West was significant for advancement. Learning a second language is a factor to progressive life both to business and society.

Communication is significant to the change. Cooperation, negotiation, sharing, listening, and emphasizing shaped emerging nations jointly into one large global community. Managers have become able to respond to the limits and consequences of everyday life with commitment, accountability, adaptability, flexibility, and integrity. Businesses have become responsive on improving the environment. It is as if everything is possible.

While trying to make changes, the pressures and complexity of business organizations skyrockets. This can be attributed to the launching of cultural differences brought in by diverse workers. Workers shift from one job to another, working part-time, as a temporary, or under contract. They no longer stay loyal to one job. I remember that until the mid-seventies, workers would stick to their jobs until retirement. In the early 1990's, as soon as the PCs were rampant, the style of employment changed. Downsizing and reorganization, hiring and firing, and retraining are common to businesses. Changes of organization culture continue to flow. Privatization, not-for-profit organizations, and contracts have become a norm. How about the attitude of workers? Will it remain the same? In an airplane terminal, this is the scenario:

A customer was negotiating business with a flight worker at the customer service section. The two were of the same ethnicity. And it went this way.

Customer: Will it be possible for me to change my passenger status so I can take advantage of the offer? Or what else can I do to get it? (The offer was to get the first flight to arrive earlier on that day to the destination.)

Flight worker: There is nothing you can do, except if the purpose of your travel is an *emergency.*

The customer was sad and was not able to say a word. A few hours later, more passengers were checking in for the flight. The customer, thinking about what the flight worker had said, spoke to another person of the same ethnicity and passed on the previous conversation. This was the answer:

Other person: The worker gave you a hint so you could have taken advantage of the offer, but you did not do anything.

Customer: What was my response supposed to be?

Other person: Hint—the purpose of your trip is an "*emergency.*" You should have been sensitive to the hint given to you, and you should have told him your trip is an emergency so that he had a reason to give you the benefit.

You will notice in this scenario that every person of the same culture also differs in attitude. The uniqueness of each might be because of the diverse geographical location, education, gender, age, religion, affiliation, and previous experience. And as they go further in their journey, their attitude also changes the job site. At this moment, the most interesting and the most powerful difference is simply when people deliver their thoughts in different ways.

I encountered the same situation in an academic institution one time. One of the employees was talking to a part-time employee.

The full-time employee said, "They are putting you in." The part-time employee listened, without giving any answer. Then the full-time employee continued, with tears in her eyes, "I don't want to lose my job." The part-time employee was surprised, but didn't say anything.

The full-time employee needed assurance that once the part-time employee got in, she would still have the job. This scenario is very common in many businesses, whether it is in the human resource office of big and small businesses; private, privatized, or government institutions; or profit or not-for-profit institutions. Communication plays a big role in hiring and firing. Sensitivity to one's emotional needs may always take you to somewhere. The part-time worker should have gotten the job, if she had used intellectual, emotional, and spiritual competency at that time.

The same is true on landing a brand-new job. Résumés, which include education and experience, are just a very minimal portion of the equation, to be qualified for the game. Other human resource people ask for "curriculum vitae" to accompany a résumé. Currently, résumé preparers make changes on résumés and experience dates are no longer included. Besides, the sensitivity of the people who surround you can be very important in this process.

In some countries, age is a criteria considered in entry level hiring. Otherwise, regardless of age, family members come first for higher position jobs. Temporary, part-time, adjunct, flexible, and other related job classifications are also open to job seekers in most countries. Currently, the loyalty of workers is almost a nightmare. Everybody is rushing to grab whatever employers offer.

The practice of hiring temps and contract workers is popular today. Current employers are convinced that temps and contract workers are what businesses need. These workers seem to manage everything from special projects to whole departments. Moreover, as a temp or contract worker, you're likely to work alongside a home engineer, accountant, doctor, lawyer, or technology expert.

Corporations in small islands like Micronesia are also willing to hire overseas workers. They hire not only blue-collar job workers, but also white-collar job workers (like accountants who might work alongside a home accountant). Job descriptions put an emphasis on "others." There is variety other projects that are available in the company. The power of "faith" works well with overseas workers, while perseverance and patience work hand in hand. A wholehearted smile works best with diverse workers.

Again, cognitive, emotional, and spiritual compatibility are important when collaborating as a team. We all understand that accounting is taught in school, but our values start from childhood and are learned as time goes by. In this situation, faith, perseverance, and patience work together.

On a small island like Palau, auto repair shops are rampant. Residents as well as contract workers buy used cars, and most of the time these end up in an auto repair shop. Usually oxygen bottles are needed in these shops. On these islands, it is understandable that there would be one oxygen bottle store. The business owner knows everybody in the island because every auto repair shop owner gets his supply from that store. Most of the time, the shop owners neglect their responsibility to return the empty bottles. After an inventory was performed, 90 percent of the empty oxygen bottles had not been returned.

Records showed the registered bottle serial numbers and the names of the shops that had them. After gathering the data needed, the store management provided a pickup utility truck and a driver, and we started the search around the island to collect the bottles. Out of those on the list, no bottle was found. Since we were not able to collect one, we continued the search in stores. In a week we were able to locate oxygen bottles in different stores.

The scenario took place in Palau in 1986, one of the islands in the Pacific. A report of completion of work was submitted to the management after a week of post inventory. All the oxygen bottles were recovered. Culture works differently in different places, and the power of faith works well. Perseverance and patience collaborated as well.

How can school administration assist instructors and students in times of complexity? The support of the lower management to instructors strengthens the instructor-student relationship in a classroom. Compassion and understanding diversity from lower management helps pump up the integrity of those involved. Again, as we always understand the theory of diversity, the practice of what we read must also be encouraged. Whatever experience and education the instructors have, they still need the lower management to support them in the classrooms. Let me tell you about these culturally diverse students. This was observed in 2010.

In a classroom where students were of different ethnicity and culture, attitude also differs. They may be the same Caucasian, the same Black, and the same Asian; and more likely born in different places, and raised in different cultures and societies. The attitude of each of these students is diverse. Ethics, most of the time varies. And this classroom is not exempted. Either, they like their instructor or not; some gave their best to participate in class activities, while others showed their discontent. However, the administration and instructors, when working together hand in hand, will have a win-win situation that includes well-designed objectives.

In this scenario, cognitive ability, emotional competency, and spiritual strength work best. On the other hand, lower-level management can be able to boost confidence and point out road maps to students to be able to navigate to their goals. While doing so, the student-instructor relationship will work at its best. Eventually, a result of a win-win goal will be accomplished: the students' success is an organization's accomplishment and can be created with a compassionate workforce.

Chapter 8

Discovering How to Change

Moving Forward

Again, we look back to 2000 BC, the discovery of different traits started, and we continue to grasp and develop in our own lives these traits, blending to what we have. The millennials, at their best, embrace what they learn from the past. Time and experience eliminates the traditional boundaries between politics, culture, technology, finance, national security, and ecology. Overseas work was freed from the government interference or regulatory practices that differ on sensitiveness from those of emerging markets.

I was in one of the islands in the Pacific in 1992 and worked in a company of three revenue centers in three different islands of Micronesia. As a worker in a place where wages were low, I was selected to handle the accounting department of the three revenue centers. I was excited working with diverse employees. Although we were in three different islands, through the use of the Internet and the click of a mouse, transactions were efficiently accomplished. The flow of communication was horizontal. Trusting one another made the work effective and possible.

Seeking Direction

Meeting the Leader's Needs of Multiple Generations

The direction of the economy, the current monetary exchange, and inflation are unpredictable. Meeting the financial needs of multiple generations depends on their social standing. People in places where you seldom find a computer seem to not be bothered by what is going on.

Traditionally, teletypes were use in communicating overseas, compared to the click of the mouse that is now used in everyday aspects of life. The current trend is faster than the wink of an eye. And most of the time, the traditionalist, baby boomers, and generation Xers, have misunderstood the fast shift of the millennials. For instance, because everything is done fast, self-righteousness, pride, and verbal criticizing become handy. And because the basic concept of leadership and learning is honesty, collaboration and cooperation, and genuine commitment, information is very easy to pass and is sometimes misunderstood. But once the receiver accepts it wholeheartedly, it can bring courage, patience, perseverance, and humbleness which are necessary in a knowledge-creating organization. Thus, leadership will be distributed among diverse individuals and teams who share responsibility for creating the organization's future. This could create a worldwide community respect, discovering the value of diversity, respecting cultural heritage, and understanding the importance of connecting people, community, and environment. With the examples of leadership from the previous generations acting as a model of high morals, the present generation is a continuation of the work of the past. Thus, the current generation traits, when linked to the previous generation's values, will not stumble. Like what Woodrow Wilson (1856-1924) said:

We grow great by dreams . . . . Some of us let these great dreams die, but others nourish and protect them; nurse them through bad days till they flourish; bring them to the sunshine and light, which comes always to those who sincerely hope that their dreams will come true.

I should say, one might not know all the words, but all have the ability to learn. Thus, mentor the younger generation and give them responsibilities. Empower them so they feel the value of work. The world goes for enrichment, so focus and get involved. Encourage passion. Lead by example. "Walk the talk." This is the cry that we hear. By practicing what we can contribute, the present and future generations with their imaginations and ideas will bring them to great success, while the past generations with their dreams, experience, and knowledge will grasp what the new generation has and can walk with them hand in hand.

Table 3: Shows the different traits of the four generations

Generation Traits

Traditionalists 1925-1945	Baby Boomers 1946-1964	Generation Xers 1965-1979	Millennials 1980-2001
Hardworking	Workaholic	Single entity	Sheltered
Loyal	Independent	Challenging work	Confident
Submissive	Goal-oriented	Freedom to manage time & work	Team-oriented
Tech-Challenged	Competitive	Feedback and recognition	Achieving
Traditional	-	-	Pressured Conventional

As I looked at the table, I noticed that a sum total of the generation traits are contributory to the process and form an effective blend to reach a goal.

In the high-stakes environment where everything is computerized and people rely on the electronic forms of communication (including composing letters or writing term papers), the traditionalists and baby boomers will finally mend the gap. Sometimes in my postgraduate class, I noticed a classmate writing her thesis in the computer, while I wrote mine on a yellow pad and typed it in the computer afterwards. A few months later, I noticed I was doing the same thing. I typed directly in the computer and did not use the yellow pad anymore. Since this is the trend, there is a prediction that in the near future, cursive writing will only be written about in history books. Using the computer, term papers, theses, dissertations, and even legal documents will become more convenient and handy.

Entrepreneurship has been practiced in the past; it was known as barter system. The concept was patterned to the previous barter practice. Regardless of one's culture, the sprouting businesses suggest that entrepreneurs have certain psychological traits.[15] The entrepreneurs know what they want and have their ideas in their head; they barely follow a prepared business plan. Currently, entrepreneurs have grown in number and became popular everywhere. Today, entrepreneurship is one source that simplifies the economic complexity. Barbecue stands are constantly seen not only in developing countries but also in industrialized countries. They can be found in sidewalks or in parking lots where travelers and commuters are commonly found.

Simple Start

From childhood to maturity, in everything we do, there is always a beginning.

When I was a child, I loved beachcombing and hiking. As I grew up, I added complex activities. I started to dream and hope that those dreams would come true.

When I had my first flight out of my country of birth, the night before was so uncomfortable. And it became worse when I was in the plane. I envy those passengers who sit down comfortably. I was so pale that I caught the attention of a flight stewardess. The stewardess said, "Please, fasten your seat belt." After saying this, she walked away. When she came back, I was still stunned and did not move at all. She noticed me and asked, "Is this your first flight?" Slowly, I answered, "Yes." Patiently, she fastened my seat belt and walked away with smile. I barely opened my lips when I said thank you.

---

[15]   A special report on entrepreneurship, (Adrian Wooldridge); *The Economist* March 14, 2009

I was so happy when I saw people snorkeling in Palau. Eight years after, I appreciated the breeze from the beautiful casuarinas in Guam. And amazingly, I noticed how disciplined those recreational fishermen were that I saw in the dock of Washington.

Winter, spring, summer, and fall, I saw people of different ethnicity on the dock to fish, or sometimes catching a few crabs and harvesting a variety of clam shells. We call them recreational fisherman because they harvest just enough for their daily consumption. And the dock is the place where people have recreation and enjoy laughter with others. The recreational fishermen may be children or adults, and of different cultures. The adult recreational fishermen follow regulations, from acquiring a license to the amount of daily harvest, while the children do it just for fun. As soon as the matured fishermen acquire a license, they can harvest forty pieces or ten pounds of smelt. This is the daily limit for them. Children are exempt from getting a license. Every time I was at the dock, I noticed them talking, laughing, and making jokes with one another; everybody seemed happy. This they can do 365 days a year. Sometimes I noticed that those who got their limits were happy sharing their catch with those who had little.

I noticed also some recreational fishermen who had more than their limit and were still trying to get more. These fishermen also could harvest other kinds of sea foods like herring, salmon, crabs, oysters, clams, and mussels. Like the smelt, there are daily limits per person. There are those who followed the regulations consistently, and some who do not. As the spiritual leaders say, self-discipline starts from the heart: "The heart is deceitful above all things, and desperately wicked: who can know it?" (Jeremiah 17:9). Because no one knows whether they got more than their limit, the recreational fishermen were free to have more until they were ready to quit.

Although we are talking of change, in this circumstance nobody could see what was in the heart of those people but them. Thus, the discipline of not taking more than their limit would be a good start. How far can people be running away from change? It is known that the heart is where emotions start, wherein discipline links understanding, knowledge, and wisdom. Once discipline starts its work, then the divine Spirit links the desire of our heart with live experience. This begins when we learn to follow simple instructions and have an inclination to follow a wider range of instructions. Thus, leadership starts from the inner self finding meaning in life focused on relationship with self and with others.

These are my experiences that attracted my interest, but they brought me discomfort and excitement. My first experience is most important; it gives a unique way of walking through my life. Thinking of my first experience brings me happiness. Thus, I decided to write simple things about others' first experiences (first day of school, first date, beginning of a marriage, etc.).

I talked with some kindergarten students on their first day of school:

Question: How do you feel on your first day to school?
Answer: I don't feel good.
Another one said: I feel sick.
Another one cried. Others shrugged their shoulders. It seemed they were all uncomfortable.

And everyone agreed that as soon as these children arrived home, though they were fed in school, they were hungry.

Joe and Marie had their first date in the restaurant:

Question: Did you enjoy the food?

Both answered: We barely touched the food.

Question: Did you have a good talk?

Both answered: No. We did not know how to start the conversation.

Morris and Mona started working today. Morris worked as a janitor, and Mona was a bank officer.

Question: Did you know your job on the first day?

Morris: No. I didn't know where and how to start.

Mona: No. I need an orientation to understand the activities of the organization.

Rowel and Pena got married. A day after the wedding day . . .

Question: How did you spend your first day?

Answer from both: We were nervous.

It seems that the first day of any new experience is really overwhelming. The first day of change feels the same. Everyone feels butterflies in their stomach. At the tender stage, fear of commitment that comes with never knowing what will happen next or maybe our self-esteem panics us.

Spiritual Leadership

While the world continues to escalate its complexities in all businesses and personal lives, spiritual leaders with their increasingly diversified organizations pass their own description of leadership that comes from within.

Tao Te Ching is one of the most powerful of all Chinese philosophic and religious texts. It has to be followed through faithful commitment and practice which starts from the heart. I read several *Tao Te Ching* quotes and selected this:

> I have three treasures which I hold and keep.
> The first is mercy; the second is economy;
> The third is daring not to be ahead of others.
> From mercy comes courage; from economy
> comes generosity; From humility comes
> leadership.
>
> Mercy brings victory in battle and
> strength in defense,
> It is the means by which heaven saves
> and guards.[16]
>
> The best athlete
> wants his opponent at his best.
> The best general
> enters the mind of his enemy.
> The best businessman
> serves the communal good.
> The best leader
> follows the will of the people.[17]

Lao Tzu emphasized that the soft overcomes the hard, as the humble conquers the proud.

---

[16] Translation by Gia Fu Feng & Jane English
[17] *Tao Te Ching*, by: Lao-Tzu; translation by. S. Mitchell (1995)

Buddhists connect ethics to spirituality. It describes love, compassion, patience, forgiveness, humility, and tolerance which are concerned with others' well-being. The Buddhist prays for a clear mind, and to stay away from greed and anger.

The Indian religious books, called Vedas, believe not only in universal tolerance, but they are actually a system of religious and philosophical practices of various cultural and language groups. They also accept that all religions are true.

The Jewish rabbis believe that God has supreme power. Meditation is their way of communing with God. They believe that pride destroys the cleanness of the heart.

The Zoroaster lived in northeastern Iran and believed in God. Zoroaster followers practice good thoughts, good deeds, and good words.

Japan's Shinto emphasizes gratitude to the *kami* (God). The Shinto is to realize and carry out the will of the kami.

Prayer is a Muslim's way to communicate with Allah. The Qur'an teaches kindness and spirituality, and is family oriented.

Christians in their walk of life pray: "Make me to understand the ways of thy precepts: so shall I talk of thy wondrous works" (Psalms 119:27 KJV).

The different organizations, with humbleness, focus on the practices and communications that bring respect to others. Discipline links their goals and commitments with understanding knowledge and wisdom.

As we look back to the beliefs of our forefathers, historians, philosophers, and religious leaders, their values seem similar to each other. The blending together comes from the inside and is practiced in our daily life, both at home and at work.

Common Traits of Different Cultures

	Believed in God	Divine Spirit	Morality	Gracious Behavior	Faithful Commitment	Practice starts from the Heart	Faith
Taoism	x	x	x	x	x	x	x
Buddhism	x	x	x	x	x	x	x
Hinduism	x	x	x	x	x	x	x
Judaism	x	x	x	x	x	x	x
Sikhism	x	x	x	x	x	x	x
Zoroastrianism	x	x	x	x	x	x	x
Shinto	x	x	x	x	x	x	x
Islam	x	x	x	x	x	x	x
Christianity	x	x	x	x	x	x	x

Table 4. Leaders of yesteryears shared the same values. They believe that the body is a vessel that glorifies God. Universal power goes beyond cultural differences. Divine Spirit, for them, is love, compassion, patience, forgiveness, humility, tolerance, sympathy, and peace to family, friends, and coworkers (chapter 1).

Chapter 9

Ready for Change

Leadership across cultures is considered foreign and not an inborn skill. It is acquired by learning. Typically, one goes for training to learn. Some consider seminars, while others pursue meditation. On the other hand, some grasp and practice what they were taught, and some don't. The process parallels the building of understanding the background of the subject.

Furthermore, those who persevere and are sincere in their endeavor have success. Since meditation is practiced openly, we may also want to understand that when meditation is not done appropriately, bad reactions take place.

Meditation

Meditation can be a tool as a personal practice to change and the acquisition of a new endeavor, which starts from the inside. It means a transformation of an objective or outlook in life. Suggested meditation starts from the heart, flowing in the spirit with a bright objective and interlinked with the mind. Our ancestors, great men and women, believed that God is the center of one's faith, and He dwells in the heart. As the objective flourishes, the process intertwines with the mind and the person feels peace inside. Before some start, they rely on external objects, such as lighting candles, as an aid to the process. Others count beads to follow a ritual. Some others meditate where they find serenity and think that a garden can fulfill that objective. Most control their breathing to ease the inner part of their spirit. Most often, meditation is cultivating a feeling of love, compassion, patience, gentleness, kindness, perseverance, and faith. Most of the time because of the complication of one's thinking, there is a problem with where and how to start meditation. I notice that the heart and spirit and mind always have a battle on whatever we want to change.

In addition to the battle of the heart and spirit, and mind, we also have our five senses that offer a wonderful rule in the process: the eyes are for seeing; from the mouth flow idioms; the ear hears every slight movement; the nose can sense all smell; and our skin is tickled with every trivial touch. The five senses can destroy the flow of meditation. May I walk you through a scenario:

It was an afternoon on a beach in Koror, Palau, where the beauty of nature is open to all. On one side was a mangrove and the other side was where people snorkel. Looking at the west where the sun goes down, the water was shallow and clear. People were free to play around or just watch the sunset. I closed my eyes and breathed deep: inhale, exhale . . . I started thinking about an objective I wanted to acquire: "love." All of a sudden a friend came near me and started talking. I was distracted and was not able to continue my concentration. Although the place was quiet where I thought peace of mind was fast to come, it was open to whoever wanted to see the beauty of nature. As a beginner, with just a slight movement my focus evaporated.

Why meditate? Practicing meditation increases creativity and patience. It develops deeper aspects of self. It is also a method for the meeting of the heart and spirit and mind so as to acquire understanding, wisdom, and knowledge. When our heart and spirit and mind acquire the desired value, we become calm and peaceful, free of worries and mental discomfort. Only then, does everything in life have a clear reason and purpose. Thus, we experience true happiness and make our life whole. Furthermore, meditation as a tool becomes a constant exercise of the heart and spirit and mind. Meditation can be a tool that prepares one to who one is today and tomorrow.

How is change linked to business and business leaders? Today's businesses or organizations are looking for balance that in addition to knowledge, moral value, and integrity, is looked upon as an asset to every leader. And meditation may be used as a tool to shape everyone's values.

In the world today where almost everything is integrated, business operations are open to the public. When one of the leaders fails, it will be the failure of the entire business. Let us look on a business that was known by every individual in business.

> Enron was well known for having a smooth flow in making profit. Stockholders and bystanders watched the growth of their stocks. At the end, it came out that some of the leaders were not honest and kept from the stockholders that the business was at that moment in turmoil. Instead of explaining to the public the problem, the leaders strategized and showed to people that the business was on good financial standing. The integrity of leaders ran dry, and the business was affected.
> —*Forbes*, 18 September 2002

Is it possible for us to meditate while walking, or in any place and at any time? Yes, it is. But for a beginner, it is suggested that it is good to start meditating in a quiet place. Meditation seems to be overwhelming. Where will one start? What specific characteristics does one want to be changed? The first day of meditation is to link the heart and spirit and mind, or as I call it, embracing a purpose through emotion and spiritual values, together with intellectual abilities is essentially advisable by staying in a quiet place. Through meditation, one can focus on something one wants to change in his life. It may be a tool used for change to sharpen or strengthen one's goal.

When change is in process, a change in the atmosphere of the body seems to change also. Honest feelings intercede, and when the inner self is emptied, it creates a vacuum in the heart allowing the Divine Spirit to move. The inner self will then be ready to progress. In an organization, this is when leaders uncover things they want to change. Their attitude towards others and self are usually changed. And then the process goes to reengineering and gradually to redesign. Eventually, a simple self-discipline arises: eliminate flexibility; self-control and compassion to understand the environment and society come into life. The courage of honest interconnection promotes the values the world embraces in common. It is when the workforce is encouraged to change. And diversity will then find unity in a group and a respect in life and heed its way to the common ground.

Differences and Similarities

Change is essential to humans. Although, people get into different practices for change, most embrace the practice of meditation (even if they practice it differently in diverse cultures). The practice of meditation is a popular tool that leads to transformation in whoever wants to pursue it. Meditation can create an inexplicable reaction in one's life. One acquires one object at a time, allowing self to let go of things that the person wants to change. Meditation started as early as the battle of David and Goliath. David's faith in his God, along with his faith and constant practice of his skill, allowed the teenage boy to win the battle (1 Samuel 17). David focused his daily life on his Creator and persistently meditated.

Lao Tzu, who lived in the sixth century BC and was one of the pioneers of the philosophy of Taoism, emphasized that "the soft overcomes the hard." Lao Tzu speaks in metaphor, and more masters followed. Just as Danny Connor with Master Michael Tse (1992) mentioned in their book:

> In the beginning there was nothing. We need something to know what is nothing; from nothing comes one. As we are attracted to heaven, we are attracted to earth. Man has to achieve balance between the two. Therefore, within man there must be a center which puts him in balance with the universe.[18]

Confucian scholars practice *qigong* (pronounced chee-gong) to improve their moral character. Taoist and Buddhist traditions use *Qigong* (*qi* which means "breath" or "energy" and *gong* which means "skill") in their meditation. *Qi* is sometimes written as *chi* and *ki* to the Japanese. Qigong practice includes meditation and the reading of a mantra (word) that helps an individual achieve its goal. Thinking of one objective assists in erasing things you want to change. Practicing meditation is letting go of everything—your possessions, your wealth, your family, your friends, and yourself, or letting go of the external world and all its desires. Thus, you clear your mind and eliminate any disturbance that occurs before the process starts. Breathing clears the mind and relaxes the body more deeply with each breath. Soon the feeling of complete freedom and peace of mind follow. Thus, feeling refreshed occurs. After the process, rubbing

---

[18]   Qigong (1992)

the hands together is suggested and then rubbing the face afterwards. It is empirical to practice often, like once in the morning and once in the afternoon to see the benefit.

In Connor's book (1992), he mentioned that while practicing ch'i, clothing should be loose and comfortable. It should also be made of natural fiber like cotton. You can experience ch'i in a house of worship, libraries, college lounges, or in any place people regularly meditate.

As it was said, (Ramaswami & Hurwitz 2006), *Yoga* is for people who have begun to inquire and search after their own souls, who have tried to focus their fickle minds, and who have been hurt by life and practiced Yoga for healing. It is also for those who want to help others, and for all of those who have no choice but to continually deal with the human condition. Breathing exercises relax the mind and give self-freedom to meditate on the change a person wants to achieve.

> Yoga is traditionally considered one of the six orthodox *darsamas* (expositions, philosophies) based on the authority of the most ancient scriptures, the Vedas.[19]

Yoga concentrates on a spiritual concept. It is related to the English word *yoke*. Yoga is defined as the union of the *jiva* (self), which may be composed of body, spirit, and mind, with the *parama* (divine). The practice of Yoga concentrates on love, truthfulness, honesty, contentment, pure mind and clean body, reading spiritual texts, and practicing by heart as an offering to God.

Jewish meditation is the beginning of a meaningful human interaction, and a deeper connection to the source of life. Meditation nourishes the

---

[19]   Yoga beneath the surface (2006)

soul. Meditation is practiced an hour before and after services. The Jewish are instructed to bow their heads to the ground until they can read the words on a coin set in front of their feet while praying. Meditation can be practiced in a group or alone. Once with a group, a mutual care and support comes up. When alone, the experience of closeness to God can add energy to the body. The study of Torah and prayer, and the celebration of holy days and life cycle events is a must before one can meditate.

When alone, one must wrap in a prayer shawl, sit with closed eyes, pray, and feel the soul as if it rises to heaven. Faith will then unite the spirit with the creator.

Like Qigong and Yoga, Hindu meditation has its own categorization. Hindu meditation focuses on spiritual enlightenment and the change of attitudes. It also seeks unification with *Brahma* (the Creature), as the perfect, spiritual truth over all existence. On a daily basis, Hindus meditate with chants (mantras), offer flowers and incense, follow ceremonial practices, and pray.

Sikhs, in India and worldwide, follow a living guru who is supposed to be a relative of Guru Gobind Singh, who was the tenth and last guru of the prophet teachers of the Sikh faith. Sikhs meditate to acquire a loving relationship with God.

Prayer is one way of meditation in Islam. Reading the Qur'an silently or out loud brings reflection on the objective in mind in which the focus is the love and gratitude to Allah (God).

While the East practiced meditation from the ancient time, in the 1970's meditation reached the West. But misunderstandings arise with participants, maybe because of differences in culture. Personal and social standing and other differences in personality are reflected in the practice of meditation.

My Time of Meditation

It was twenty-four years ago, in Micronesia, when a missionary (everybody called him Pastor Tad) emphasized a verse: "But seek ye first the kingdom of God, and his righteousness; and all these things shall be added unto you" (Matthew 6:33 KJV). My heart was sad and my mind started to get wary. It gave me sleepless nights, until one day, I noticed myself praying, asking God to help me "seek Your Kingdom." And deep inside, crying, I asked how I could do that. Suddenly I realized that I was in the process of meditation. And finally, I prayed and thought about it day and night, thanking our Creator for starting the process in me. Henceforth, I continued learning how to seek His Kingdom, and I practiced my faith. Faith, that before I knew it, was a part of my being. From then on, I learned to live on a day-to-day basis, hoping that the following day would bring grace to everyone. As it was written in Psalms 63:3 (KJV), "When I remember thee upon my bed, and meditate on thee in the night watches."

On the first days of meditation, truth unbalanced me. One situation I encountered was forgiveness, both to others and to me. The distrustful resistance in my heart was activated, and my brain opposes more. At that very moment, I didn't know if I was ready to continue. But I was determined to seek out the pain of conversion. Many scenarios came to my mind that made me cry; my ego was hurt. But still, I must forgive. This is when the following circumstances came to my mind.

Businesses and organizations are alike in one thing. Both look for a way to expand. It may be as affiliates, joint ventures, extensions of the main office, or international networking. Services are usually networked. It is a common practice that people ask assistance from friends. And businesses and organizations are not free from the practice. Let us see how a business worked with an organization.

In this scenario, both the business president and the organization vice president were friends. The one man had a business in a location where his friend wanted to put up an extension to his organization. Before I go further, "business" as used in this scenario is considered "for profit" and the organization is a "not for profit." As friends, the president assisted the organization to start putting together a building and a permit to operate. Both were excited to complete the job. The work was completed at minimal working hours and at low cost. The existing business workers were familiar with the type of work, and they accomplished the task in an efficient manner. The workers felt they had done the right thing. But when the work was presented to the organization, it was criticized. The workers of the existing business were stunned; they tried to understand what they had done wrong. The help was sincere. Eventually, they learned it was protocol the organization was looking for. Then, a question arose. Did they need protocol to do those simple works? How would they help next time? Deep inside, knew they had to consider the differences and do the right thing. The differences in perception between the business and the organization affected the work of each group.

As Michel de Montaigne (1600) mentioned, a perception might be acceptable in one place and not acceptable in the other place. On the other hand, Kant (1747-1770)[20] in his argument, emphasized perceptions as subjective.

---

[20] His metaphysical ideas, particularly those of his pre-critical period are stunning, (Beck 1969, 433).

One day I found myself on a journey where my timeline depended on the obedience of my heart and spirit and mind. One day at a time, after twenty-four years of meditation, I learned to love. It was an extraordinary experience to love those that I didn't like before, those I believed had done wrong to people I love. Then time made me understand that there is an encouraging purpose for everything. And that is when I learned to look on the other side of the fence.

Eventually, I achieved peace and joy. Patience and kindness came next—one at a time. And it feels relaxing to be patient and kind. It feels good that my heart, spirit, and mind intertwine on the purpose I am meditating for. Understanding the walk of life humbled me. Praises and blessings to my Creator; He teaches me the value of life. I turned out to be simple and flexible; my complexity vanished. Little by little, the barrier (pride) shrank and was purged.

While one is committed to change, the heart and spirit and mind link together to change one's attitude as a person. This applies also to business organizations whose aspiring leaders work tirelessly as they collaborate to reconfigure and redesign as they improve their organization's trustworthiness to service. Sooner, the perseverance of the leader gets the attention of the workforce and they become committed and collaborative to reach both the company and personal goals. With my own definition, "committed" includes "trustworthiness," and "collaborative workforce" includes "honesty and humility."

Most businesses and organizations are giving leadership training for change. How will this solve the problem of economic uncertainty to integrated nations? The greatest excitement is when two leaders of different nations merge. Will these leaders have a sense of balance to their differences? Let me walk you through this story that I heard from my daughter, Rhodora.

> There are two fields, and a fence divides these fields. On the one side of the fence, the grass was short and some parts were dry. While on the other side, the grass was green and robust. A horse was standing in the dry field, near the fence. The horse put up his head, looking over the fence and intently watching the green grass. Then the horse gently put his head through the fence and started eating the green grass from the other side. As soon as he was full, he gently put up his head and turned around.

> There was silence for a while. Then I added, "So the grass was not trampled; instead it was aerated. This would even make the grass grow faster and thicker." With smile, my daughter said, "Yes."

The good news is that the West and East have something in common. They believe that they are all created by God. Furthermore, meditation originated in the East, back to the ancient times; in the 1970's it became popular in the West. It is not only a religious practice, but it is practiced for the health benefit (*Journal of Transpersonal Psychology* 1970). It is a simple process, and those committed for change are excessively confident that they will be able to turn their goal into reality. While continuing my journey, I learned to forgive and practiced great tolerance, continuously; humbleness came next. After these long years of self-discipline, meditation became a part of my daily life. And I do it any time of the day, and anywhere that my heart and spirit collide, while my mind collaborates. Self-discipline interlinks the heart and spirit, and mind; that produces wisdom, understanding, and knowledge.

Table 5: Self-discipline interlinks the heart and spirit, and mind; that produces wisdom, understanding, and knowledge.

Moving on to the next level, meditation even during travel or at work, at home or everyplace is possible. This next level is more comfortable. The heart always has time to meditate. Through the process, there is freedom and honesty in communication. Meditation as a tool becomes a continuous process. Change is fragile and develops slowly. Forgiving self is as important as forgiving others. While in process, I thank our Creator with a grateful heart and spirit, and mind. Meditation in this book is focused on the Divine Spirit, which to our forefathers is love, patience, forgiveness, gentleness, humility, tolerance, sympathy; peace to family, friends, and in the workplace. The process works on one objective at a time. Commitment and perseverance always come together as ingredients to the fulfillment of change.

After a few years of meditation, I noticed a change when my heart and spirit and mind collaborated. It was a collision of cognitive and emotional and spiritual gifts. Furthermore, a peace of mind follows.

The Challenge

Can we change our perspective? Many times, we try what will work to get away from our self-centeredness. While change can be overwhelming and challenging, meditation in its mysterious way helps maximize the grip of an objective to change. As a start, the five senses play a large part because even the slightest noise can get you out of focus. Closing your eyes, the natural smells and taking deeper breaths (inhale-exhale) usually brings tranquility. A delicate touch startles you and will make you look around. Thus, besides discipline on breathing, discipline on seeing, hearing, smelling, and touching is also vital.

The change of perspective is what we are looking for: a generous love that is full of promise. While we let discipline work in us, change develops. We need one objective at a time to start down the path to the life we always wanted to acquire in our journey. At the time of meditation, we let go of the past, crushed barren behavior, forgot the complexities, and focused on our objective to use in our daily life. In the moment of meditation, the thoughts to change should overcome our weaknesses. Let those negative thoughts melt. And as the negative thoughts were put aside, be reminded that you have changed. Once you notice the negative thoughts from others, just do the right thing. Now, you have acquired understanding, knowledge, and wisdom, the tools you can use in your daily life as a good citizen or as an effective leader. As we are committed to change, meditation can be a good start to make us a new person. In this book, I focus on *love, patience, forgiveness, gentleness, humility, tolerance, sympathy, and peace to family, friends, and in the workplace.*

Perseverance and commitment form one facet to reach our goal. As we are committed and persevere, the process of meditation will come smooth. Meditate on the objective that leads you to be patient, humble, forgiving, gentle, sympathetic, compassionate, and peaceful with family, friends, and in the workplace. And for the fulfillment of all these, we must be filled with our faith, and let the Divine Spirit guide us throughout.

In time of change, we persevere on what we really aspire to be. We open up the essence of our heart. While in process, we try to close our

79

eyes and hold our breath (inhale-exhale). Do this until we are able to calm ourselves down, then we can focus. We become aware of the reality that we want a change in our life.

Through meditation with a desire in our heart, we change. Meditation then is an emotion that leads to the deeper feeling of our heart: our spirit. It is when our heart and spirit are in a very quiet moment that they collaborate with our thoughts. With collaboration, we persevere and commit.

Listening to a child can help us understand how to think like a child. The naive attitude of a child leads to a clear and honest perception. One time, I was talking with my half-Korean granddaughter. I said, "Let's do yoga." She said, "I'll lead." This is how it goes: My granddaughter continued, "Let's lie down, close our eyes, and think that violets surround us. We smell violets now. Eeeemmmm . . . It is so good. We feel calm. We have peace of mind. We are calm. Think of the things you want to be . . . Breath deep, relax and enjoy . . ." As the process went on, it seemed that we saw violets blooming around us, and we smelled the fragrance, feeling free to use our own creativity and wisdom.

This was from a five-year-old girl. Every detail of her words carried us away because of the clear and direct perception that the little girl inspired. From this point I felt empty inside. I experienced the inner change that was supposed to happen in that moment. Through the meeting of the heart and spirit, and mind, my mode of thinking was changed. If we can only think like a child, since our heart and spirit, and mind has been molded, then and only then will we have a clear perception of change.

Meditation is suggestive to be applicable to business and organization leaders too. Looking high on the cognitive ability of an individual, emotional competence and spiritual being is suggestive to work together to get away from one's self-centeredness. This way of collaboration works correctly.

Change and meditation can be said to be a part of a history. It is said that meditation comes to clarity only when we see clearly the ever-changing circumstances in our lives. This was true of the lives of Esau and Jacob.[21] As we follow the journey of Esau, although blunders happened with his brother in the past, Jacob's meditation brought him humility that melted the heart of Esau, who forgot his anger. Esau forgave and had reconciliation with his brother.

People have different attitudes on taking things, and they show different ways to change. Some in a short period of time grasp it and change; others take months or even years before they can even start thinking of change. To every individual, change moves his or her life in a different manner. The process of meditation varies, according to our faith. The fulfillment of the desire to change will give comfort to one to listen to others, ourselves, and most of all to the Divine Spirit. We learn to balance our daily walk in life—at home, work, and in society. We learn to do the right thing in every step of our way and to our global community. The Divine Spirit guides us through.

As we complete the journey, love, patience, forgiveness, gentleness, humility, tolerance, sympathy; peace to family, friends, and in the workplace are being practiced in our daily life.

---

[21] BBCoakharbor, Pastor Robert Sargent, May 2011.

The Present and Future Generations

In a world with continuous change, a wide variety of changing circumstances revolve every now and then. Most of us, (traditionalists, baby boomers, generation Xers, and millennials), including those in the business world, expect a quick fix to problems. Overwhelmed as they are, they allow themselves to be taken away by their emotions and thoughts of a profit from the short-term moves of leadership. Others are patiently waiting, hoping that the process brings a result they expected. While most are on stand-by, others' (mostly the millennials) ideas overflow the market, knowing it will elevate the society, environment, and the neighboring countries. While the millennials are busy exploring, some traditionalists, baby boomers, and generation Xers contribute their expertise and experience joining the millennials to rebuild, reconfigure, and reengineer business and organizations. Most of the time, the process of reaching goals is not smooth, and hence, it is wise to remain committed and consistent. While a nation's culture and tradition has a strong hold on everyone in the community, to minimize reconfiguration and reconstruction, we should challenge ourselves for change to provide opportunity to the purpose.

While Christopher Columbus (1451-1506)[22] said the world was round, Thomas L. Friedman (2005)[23] made the popular statement that the world is flat. Columbus and Friedman had two different perspectives that linked politics, culture, technology, finance, national security, and ecology and changed the thinking of almost everyone and the global business as well. The ideas of the philosophers Socrates, Plato, and Aristotle are continuously applied hypothetically and rationally. The thinkers Michel de Montaigne (1600) and Immanuel Kant's (1724-1804) thinking was

---

[22] Explorer, colonizer, and navigator

[23] An award-winning *New York Times* columnist.

rewritten and passed on, until Daniel Goleman (1995)[24] wrote his book *Emotional Intelligence*, and Reuben Bar-On (2000) started quantifying emotional ability. Furthermore, as the millennials, joined by some traditionalists, baby boomers, generation Xers, walked hand in hand, they showed faith and hope in God. Thus, adding the spiritual compatibility to the equation, and the ingredients of change are complete. Eventually, cognitive ability and emotional ability and spiritual being were interlinked and quantified. Theoretically, the world is connected geographically, and to trade as well. This big change we enjoy gives us the freedom to compete and collaborate, wherever we are, whoever we are, and with our ideas, we excel.

Furthermore, as the teachings of Confucius, (551-479 BC), a moral teacher who witnessed the beginning of Taoism, Buddhism, and the beginning of Greek philosophy, spread in different nations, the teaching of other nations, Hinduism, Judaism, Sikhism, Zoroastrianism, Shinto, Islam, and Christianity are also practiced as well. In spite of all these practices, it is suggestive to respect cultural differences and improve similarities, pushing to create a peaceful relationship. Training is vital to everyone, maybe academically and workshops, or maybe meditation.

Most if not all millennials adopted the cognitive, emotional, and spiritual competence in their daily life and linked it to trade. But how much of each (cognitive, emotional, and spiritual) are needed to be effective? Let us examine some survey statements and find out our strengths and weaknesses. Find out by yourself how much we need change. The survey statement will allow everyone to understand that compassion, patience, understanding, kindness, gentleness, humbleness, and faith are vital to our daily life.

---

[24]   Author, psychologist, and science journalist

A Pinch of Your Thoughts

This survey asks about attitude and your inner thoughts. Give your answer to each question, depending on your perception. Every answer will be measured on four categories: "strongly agree," "agree," "strongly disagree," and "disagree." Your answers explain how your heart and spirit, and mind interlink. There is no wrong answer.

- Put an "X" in the box to the left of your answer.

1. I learn to love what I am resisting, then when I might likely meet others of a different appearance, I will most likely love them without hesitation.
   - ○ Strongly agree
   - ○ Agree
   - ○ Disagree
   - ○ Strongly disagree

2. I can say that good sales management is activities management.
   - ○ Strongly agree
   - ○ Agree
   - ○ Disagree
   - ○ Strongly disagree

3. I am motivated and directly controlled by my managers.
   - ○ Strongly agree
   - ○ Agree
   - ○ Disagree
   - ○ Strongly disagree

4. I can be a leader, because leadership can be learned at any age if the commitment to learn is present.

    O Strongly agree

    O Agree

    O Disagree

    O Strongly disagree

5. I have self-discipline.

    O Strongly agree

    O Agree

    O Disagree

    O Strongly disagree

6. To succeed, I need to bring my highest; most spiritual self to work each day.

    O Strongly agree

    O Agree

    O Disagree

    O Strongly disagree

7. I am continuously finding ways to astonish my customers.

    O Strongly agree

    O Agree

    O Disagree

    O Strongly disagree

8. My past has nothing to do with my desire to change.

    O Strongly agree

    O Agree

    O Disagree

    O Strongly disagree

9. My thought has nothing to do to my feelings regarding accepting an objective.
    - O Strongly agree
    - O Agree
    - O Disagree
    - O Strongly disagree

10. I can be a leader, because I am compassionate and know how to get great results from my people by managing their feelings.
    - O Strongly agree
    - O Agree
    - O Disagree
    - O Strongly disagree

11. The Divine Spirit guides me not only in my spiritual life, but also in my daily life.
    - O Strongly agree
    - O Agree
    - O Disagree
    - O Strongly disagree

12. My heart and spirit, and mind work together to have complete change.
    - O Strongly Agree
    - O Agree
    - O Disagree
    - O Strongly disagree

13. In the first stage of meditation, I struggle making my heart and spirit collaborate with my mind.
    - ○ Strongly Agree
    - ○ Agree
    - ○ Disagree
    - ○ Strongly disagree

14. I meditated and practiced the change in my life.
    - ○ Strongly Agree
    - ○ Agree
    - ○ Disagree
    - ○ Strongly disagree

15. I can say; I'm spiritually mature when I can see both sides of the fence, understand the difference, and do the right thing.[25]
    - ○ Strongly agree
    - ○ Agree
    - ○ Disagree
    - ○ Strongly disagree

---

1. SA; 2. SD: Good sales management is outcome management. 3. SD: Managers can't directly control their people. Motivation comes from within. 4. SA; 5. SD: Use self-discipline. It is a skill. 6. SA; 7. SA; 8. SA; 9. SD: My thought has something to do with my feelings regarding accepting an objective. 10. SD: I can be a leader because I am compassionate and

---

[25] Survey was based from: "9 lies that are holding your business back," by Steve Chandler and San Beckford. *100 Ways to Motivate Others* by Steve Chandler and Scott Richardson (2005), Career Press, Inc., Franklin Lakes, N.J. and from my spiritual understanding.

can seek creative input in their direct reports, which is motivational for the manager and the subordinate. 11. SA. 12. SA. 13. SA. 14. SA. 15. SA.

Continually, millennials take high risk in their walk; either they think as an ordinary citizen or as a trader. They are confident that while a nation's culture and tradition has a strong hold in every community, the refinement of life depends on having peace with God. Keep God's Word and practice it in one's daily life, allowing the Divine Spirit to extend love, compassion, gentleness, patience, humbleness, perseverance, and faith to develop in us. In our daily life, the practice of these things is a long nurturing to self: heart and spirit, and mind. The human inner conflict is a conflict between the indwelling Spirit of God and the unquenchable ego (self); between surrender to the power of self and the full display of power of God in the heart and spirit, and mind. In this writing, I focus on *love, patience, forgiveness, gentleness, humility, tolerance, sympathy, and peace to family, friends, and in the workplace.*

References

Abram, I. (2002). *What It Means to Be Jewish: The Voices of Our Heritage.* (1st ed.), New York: St. Martin's Press.

Adler, M. J. (1978). *Aristotle for Everybody.* (1st ed.), New York: Touchtone Rockefeller Center.

Alson, R (2008). *The Trophy Kids Grow Up: How the Millennial Generation Is Shaking Up the Workplace.* (1st ed.), San Francisco, CA: HE Printing.

Ankeri, G. (2000). *Global Communication without Universal Civilization.* INU Societal research. vol. 1: *Coexisting Contemporary Civilizations: Arabo-Muslim, Bharati, Chinese, and Western.* Interuniversity Institute, CH-1211 Geneva-ll, Switzerland, U.S.A.: MIT, Cambridge, MA: INU Press.

Aronson, B. H. (2004). *Buddhist Practice on Western Ground: Reconciling Eastern Ideals and Western Psychology.* Boston, Massachusetts: Shambhala Publications, Inc., retrieved 17 March 2011, www. shambhala.com from Google.

Bar-On, R. (2000). *Emonet Digest 403.* Academic articles and abstracts. Retrieved July 22, 2006, from http://eqi.org/acad 1.htm.

Bass, B. M. (1985). *Leadership and Performance beyond Expectations.* New York: The Free Press.

Beck, B. M. (1960). *A Commentary on Kant's Critiques of Practical Reason.* Chicago: University

Bennet, S. (2007). *Wisdom Walk.* Novato, CA: New World Library.

Bourgeault, C. (2008). *The Wisdom Jesus, Transforming Heart and Mind—A New Perspective on Christ and His Message.* Massachusetts: Shambhala Publications, Inc.

Bowker, J. W. (1997). *Shinto, World Religion.* (1st American ed.), New York: DK Publishing, Inc.

Bstan-'dzin-rgya-mtsho, (1999). *Ethics for the New Millennium, His Holiness; The Dalai Lama.* New York: Riverhead Books.

Carroll, C. (2002). *The New Faithful: Why Young Adults are Embracing Christian Orthodoxy.* Chicago, Illinois: Loyola Press.

Cavalier, R. (1997). *Plato for Beginners.* New York: Writers and readers publishing, Inc.

Chan, D. W. (2007). *Leadership and Intelligence.* Roeper Review (2007, Spring) 29, 3, 183-189, 7p, 2 charts (art.abstract), Hong Kong, China. Retrieved June 11, 2007, from EBSCOHost.

Chapman, G., and Thomas, J. (2006). *The Five Languages of Apology; How to Experience*

Healing in All Your Relationships. Chicago, IL: by permission of Zondervan Publishing House. By permission, Northfield Publishing.

Chiang, M., Huang, T. (2005). *The Secret Teachings of the Tao Te Ching.* Vermont: Destiny Books.

Chobanian, E. (2005). *Real Spirit: Fun Ideas for Refreshing, Relaxing, and Staying Strong.* Middleton, WI: Pleasant Company Publications.

Chopra, D. & Simon, D. (2004). *The Seven Spiritual Laws of Yoga: A Practical Guide to Healing Body, Mind, and Spirit.* Hoboken, New Jersey: Published by John Wiley & Sons, Inc. Published simultaneously in Canada.

Chuckrow, R. (1998). *The Tai Chi Book. Refining and Enjoying a Lifetime of Practice. Including the Teachings of Cheng Man-ch'ing, William C.C. Chen, and Harvey I. Sober.* Boston, MA: YMAA Publishing Center.

Cohn-Sherbok, D. (2002). *The Wisdom of the Kabbalah.* Oxford OX2 7AR, England: Compiled, Oneworld Publications. © 2002, Berne Convention, 185 Banbury Road, Oxford OX2 7AR, England.

Connor, D. (1992). *Qigong, Featuring Master Michael Tse; Chinese Movement & Meditation for Health.* © 1992, Danny Connor. Boston, MA/York Beach, ME, Boston, MA 02210, WeiserBooks.

Drucker, P. (2006). *Classic Drucker. "The Man Who Invented Management."* Boston, MA: Harvard Business School Publishing Corporation.

Duncan, R. (2005). *Gandhi Selected Writings, Mohandas Gandhi.* Boston & New York: Beacon Press & Dover Publications.

Freidman, T. L. (2006). *The World Is Flat: A Brief History of the Twenty-First Century.* New York: Farrar, Straus and Giroux.

Fukuyama, F. (1995). *Trust.* New York: The Free Press.

Gardner, H. (1983). *Frames of Mind: The Theory of Multiple Intelligence. What Is Intelligence?* New York: Basic Books.

Goleman, D. (1995). *Emotional Intelligence.* New York: Bantam Books.

Hackett, C. F. (2007). *A Comparative Study of Emotional Intelligence between Leader/Managers of the Philippines and United States.* Dissertation, 2008, Argosy University, CA.

Harrison, P. (2001). *A Complete Guide to Discovering Meditation.* London, WCIB 3JH: Caxton Publishing Group.

Hasan, A. G. (2009). *Red, White, and Muslim: My Story of Belief.* New York: HarperCollins Publishers.

Hofstede, G., and Hofstede, G.J. (1997). *Culture & Organizations; Software of the Mind (Reviewed and Expanded) Intercultural Cooperation and Its Importance for Survival.* New York: McGraw-Hill.

Hormats, R. D. (2003). "Abraham Lincoln and the Global Economy." *Harvard Business Review*, 00178012, Aug. 2003, vol. 81, issue 8. Database: Business Source Premier.

Huntington, P. S. (1996). *The Clash of Civilizations and the Remaking of World Order.* New York: Touchtone Rockefeller Center.

Kolodiejchuk, B. (2007). *Mother Teresa, Come Be My Light. The Private Writings of the "Saint of Calcutta."* New York, London, Toronto, Sydney, Auckland: Doubleday.

Lama Surya Das, (2007). *Buddha Is as Buddha Does.* New York: HarperCollins Publishers.

Legge, J., trans. *The Path of Virtue; The Illustrated Tao Te Ching; Lao Tzu.* New York: China, an imprint of Harry N. Abrams, Inc. Retrieved 04 April, 2011, www.abrambooks.com, from Google.

Leloup, J. (2000). *Compassion and Meditation: The Spiritual Dynamic between Buddhism and Christianity.* Translated by Joseph Rowe, 2009. Inner traditions, Vermont.

Lenhard, J. (2004). *Scepticism and Mathematization; Pascal and Pierce on Mathematical Epistinology. Philosophica 74 (2004) pp. 85-102.* Retrieved 17 April 2011: from Google.

Liu, D. (1986). *T'ai Chi Ch'uan and Meditation.* New York: Schocken Books.

McSweeney, B. (2002). Dr. Geert Hofstede Cultural Dimensions, Hofstede's Model of National Cultural Differences and their consequences: A triumph of faith—a failure of analysis. Retrieved 17 March 2004: from Google.

Milgram, G. (2011). *Introduction to Jewish Meditation.* Retrieved 02 March 2011, http://www.reclaimingjudaism.org/prayer/meditatin. htm, from Google.

Musleah, R., and R. M. Klayman. (1997). *Sharing Blessings. Children's Stories for Exploring the Spirit of the Jewish Holidays.* Woodstock, Vermont: Jewish Lights Publishing.

Navia, L. E. (2007). *Socrates, A Life Examined.* New York: Prometheus Book, Aseherst.

New International Version, (1973, 1978, 1984). *Holy Bible.* Philippines: Manila International Bible Society.

Nigosan, S.A. (1993). *The Zoroastrian Faith.* © McGill-Queen's University Press, 1993. Printed in Canada,

Odier, D. (1974). *Meditation Techniques of the Buddhist & Taoist Masters.* translated by John Mahoney, Inner traditions, © 1974 by editors Robert Laffont, translation, © 1986, 2003 by Inner Traditions International.

Pascal, B. (1600). *Pensees.* Translated by W. F. Trotter—Section I, "Thoughts on mind and on style—essays by Michel de Montaigne." Retrieved: 17 April 2011; www.oregonstate.edu/instruct/phl302/texts/pascal/pensees-a.txt, from Google.

Ramaswami, S, & Hurwitz, D. (2006). *Yoga beneath the Surface.* New York: An Imprint of Avalon Publishing Group, Inc.

Revised King James, (1611). *The Holy Bible.* Washington: Church Publishing.

Rosen, S. (2000). *The Examined Life Reading from Western Philosophy from Plato to Kant:*

Immanuel Kant. Copyright 2000 by Stanley Rosen. Random House Reference, New York.

Ruggiero, A. (2006). Judaism. Edited by Adriane Ruggiero. Copyright © 2006 by Thomson Gale. Greenhaven Press, MI

Selby, J. (2004). *Meditation the Cool Way to Calm: Solve Your Problems, Find Peace of Mind, and Discover the Real You.* Boston, MA: Tuttle Publishing.

Sikh Missionary Society (2003). "Literary value of the poetry of the gurus." Retrieved 14 April 2011 from info@sikhmissionarysociety.org.

Strathern, P. (1997). *Socrates in 90 Minutes.* Chicago: Ivan R. Dee, Inc.

The Holy Bible, (KJV). The text conformable to that of the edition of 1611. Church Publishing, Oak Harbor, WA.

The Oxford Dictionary of World Religions, (1997). "Sikhism. Zoroastrianism". New York: Oxford University Press.

Whitney, J. O. (1996). *The Economic of Trust.* New York: McGraw-Hill.

Young, S. (2007). *Hinduism.* New York: Marshall Cavendish Benchmark.

Notes

These Can Be Learned:

- Love, compassion, perseverance, patience, forgiveness, humility, tolerance, gentleness, kindness, peace to family, peace in the workplace

Other Things to Know:

- Hard people: People who are firm or solid in their decision
- Committed: One who follows through, no matter what
- Interested: One who does something only at his convenience
- Persistence: Mental and behavioral toughness
- Self-discipline: A skill

Great Memories

Twenty-five years ago I traveled with my ten children from the Philippines. Although my dream was to be in the United States with my children, we landed on a small island of Micronesia—Koror, Palau. After eight long years of employment in Palau, I was given an opportunity to work in Guam (a territory of United States). I and my children transferred to Guam. Eventually, my dream came true.

I worked in different firms (government, privatized, not-for-profit, and for-profit), with workforce of diverse cultures. I learned serving the community with integrity.

Eventually, we were settled in the United States. After all the hardship, the path to higher education was opened to me. And continually, I pursued my master's degree in business administration (MBA), at Argosy University, Orange County. And I completed my doctorate degree in business administration (DBA) at the same school, with an emphasis on international trade and international business, respectively. Before I go further, I would like to note also that I completed my undergraduate studies (BSC accounting), at Far Eastern University, Manila, Philippines.

In 2009, I started FocusnNEWS, LLC and Focus*n*NEWS, Research, a profit and not-for-profit organization. The long process taught me perseverance, patience, and gentleness. I learned to be calm and humble. Love continues to grow in my heart. I hope that tomorrow brings grace to everyone. Faith brought us far.